ANSV

101 QUESTIONS (

Also published by Geoffrey Chapman

Responses to 101 Questions on the Bible: Raymond E. Brown SS
Responses to 101 Questions on the Dead Sea Scrolls:
  Joseph A. Fitzmyer SJ
Responses to 101 Questions on Feminism: Denise Lardner Carmody

Rowanne Pasco

ANSWERS TO
101 QUESTIONS
ON THE CATECHISM

GEOFFREY
CHAPMAN

Geoffrey Chapman
A Cassell imprint
Wellington House, 125 Strand, London WC2R 0BB

First published 1995

British Library Cataloguing-in-Publication Data
A catalogue record for this book is available from the British Library.

ISBN 0–225–66766–5

Nihil obstat: David McLoughlin, Censor Deputatus
Imprimatur: Monsignor Ralph Brown, VG
Westminster
7 December 1994

The *Nihil obstat* and *Imprimatur* are official declarations that a book or pamphlet is
free of doctrinal or moral error. No implication is contained therein that those who
have granted the *Nihil obstat* and *Imprimatur* agree with the contents, opinions or
statements expressed.

Typeset by Colset Typesetters Limited, UK
Printed and bound in Great Britain by Biddles Ltd, Guildford and King's Lynn

CONTENTS

PREFACE

The long-awaited *Catechism of the Catholic Church* is an amazing achievement, involving six years of work and hundreds of minds from all over the world. It is a text containing many treasures but, as with the pearl of great price of Jesus' story, these treasures demand persistent digging if they are to be unearthed. Much of the Catechism is very difficult to understand for the general reader, because it is aimed, first and foremost, at bishops and catechists, and contains many complex theological and philosophical concepts, expressed in technical language.

Despite considerable difficulties with language, the Catechism has already become a best-seller, showing that there is great hunger for knowledge of the faith. During my ten years as editor of *The Universe*, I was often struck by this hunger. It is not that people reject Christianity; they simply do not know what it is. Too often church documents, in spite of the richness of their teaching, go unread because of the way they are written.

Those who have produced the Catechism recognize this problem and simplified versions of its teachings will be needed. They have asked that this should be done.

This book of questions and answers on the Catechism is a response to this request. None of the teachings has been changed, they are just presented in what I hope is simple language.

The Catechism of the Council of Trent, often quoted in the new Catechism, addressed itself to the 'Friendly Reader'. I have tried to keep this in mind.

The numbers in brackets at the ends of paragraphs are a guide to where this subject is dealt with in the *Catechism of the Catholic Church*. They are paragraph numbers, not page numbers.

Rowanne Pasco
July 1994

Extracts from the
Pastoral Letter
of His Eminence,
Cardinal Basil Hume,
on the occasion of the publication of
the English-language version of the
Catechism of the Catholic Church

Today we need a clear, up-to-date and authoritative summary of
Catholic teaching. The new Catechism is precisely that. It will help
us all to know our Catholic faith better and to explore its saving truths
more fully. It will be welcomed by many adult Catholics who want
to know more about their faith. It will assist parents in their responsibility to teach the truths of our faith to their children, governors and
teachers in our schools, catechists in our parishes and priests in their
ministry of teaching and preaching. It will also guide us in our contacts
and discussions with fellow Christians of other traditions. It will be
a key document for all engaged in the task of handing on the faith.

The Catechism is an authoritative summary of Catholic teaching. It
comes to us with the authority of the Holy Father himself. This is important. It distinguishes this Catechism from other summaries of the faith,
or catechisms, which have appeared in recent years. An important part
of our faith is that divine assistance is given to the successor of St Peter,
the Pope, and to the bishops, successors of the apostles, when they for-
mulate the faith of the Church in their teaching. This Catechism was
given to us by the Pope after consultation with all the bishops of the
world.

No summary of Catholic teaching can be exhaustive. Human words
will always be inadequate in expressing the divine truths they seek to con-
vey.... But when the Catechism is read and studied with the eyes of
faith, we go beyond the limits of concept and language to contemplate,
or glimpse, something about God and his purposes, which the Spirit
within us will enable us to see.

We must receive this Catechism with respect and gratitude. We welcome it as a historic and timely contribution to the life of the Church.

PROLOGUE

Q.1 What is the *Catechism of the Catholic Church*?

A. The Catechism describes itself as a unified 'presentation of the Catholic Faith in its entirety', and its several hundred pages summarize contemporary church teaching. In his introduction, Pope John Paul calls it 'A sure norm for teaching the faith'. It is described as universal because it applies to the whole Church in every part of the world. Although the Catechism exists in many translations, the contents remain the same because the teaching of the Catholic Church is the same in every country.

The word 'catechism' has been used in the Church for centuries to describe a teaching process, a passing-on of the faith. It comes from the Greek *katechein* which means 'to instruct orally' or 'to shout down'. The most common form of catechism in the past was as a series of questions and answers. This new version is not presented this way, but simply as a series of paragraphs, each setting out various aspects of church teaching.

Over the centuries many catechisms have been produced by the Church, but the only other universal catechism was that compiled after the Council of Trent (1545–63). It was called 'The Catechism for the Curates', and was specifically aimed at the clergy, many of whom at that time lacked formal theological training. It is also known and referred to as 'the Roman Catechism' because it was compiled mainly by senior church figures in Rome.

The new *Catechism of the Catholic Church* is the work of cardinals, bishops and other experts from around the world. Such a variety of talents have been involved that the Pope in his introduction calls it 'a symphony of faith'.

The Council of Trent came at a turbulent time for the Church as it battled with the Reformation. The idea for the new Catechism is also rooted in a challenging and dramatic time: that of the Second Vatican Council which was opened in 1962 by Pope John XXIII. During a special meeting of bishops in Rome called by Pope John Paul II in 1985 to mark the twentieth anniversary of the closing of the council, delegates spoke of the need for a new catechism reflecting the teaching of that council. The Pope backed the idea and set up a committee to start the work, under the chairmanship of Cardinal Ratzinger, head of the Vatican Congregation for the Doctrine of the Faith.

The aim of the new Catechism is to help bishops in their ministry and to renew the life of the whole Church in the spirit of Vatican II. The original Roman Catechism defined the purpose of teaching the faith: '... the love of the Lord must always be made accessible, so that anyone can see that all the works of perfect Christian virtue spring from love and have no other objective than to arrive at love.' The new Catechism is based on sources from many ages; the Bible, the saints, the liturgies of Eastern and Western Christianity, church councils, especially Vatican II, the Roman Catechism, and the teaching of many Popes. Sacred tradition, sacred Scripture and the Magisterium of the Church are all so connected that one cannot stand without the other. Guided by the one Holy Spirit, they all contribute to the salvation of souls.

The Catechism is essentially a reference text aimed at those responsible for teaching the Catholic faith. It is important to realize what it is not. In their commentary on the text, the Catholic bishops of England and Wales point out that in its statements about morality, for instance, the Catechism only presents an overview of central and sure teaching for adult readers and does not deal with individual moral questions in detail or provide any full response to recent complex moral questions which are still under discussion. Nor is the catechism intended for children, written as it is in language that is at times technical and difficult. Neither does it represent any change in church doctrine, or an analysis of current theology. It is not trying to defend or prove Catholic belief, but simply to set it out with certainty and authority.

Q.2 Why has this catechism been produced? Does it mean that the Church's teaching has changed?

A. This new Catechism has been produced because four hundred years have passed since the last universal catechism, which was produced after the Council of Trent in the sixteenth century. Much has changed in the life of human beings and of the Church since then. People are faced with different situations and new questions; for example, the development of nuclear weapons or the possibility of 'test-tube babies'. Dramatic changes have taken place in the Church, particularly after the Second Vatican Council. One of the most evident of these was seen in the Mass. For centuries this had been celebrated in Latin by a priest with his back to the congregation which took little active part in the proceedings.

Nowadays, thanks to Vatican II, the laity play a far greater role including, for example, reading from Scripture, leading some of the prayers and helping to distribute Holy Communion as lay ministers. Other changes are seen in the greater and growing friendship between Roman Catholics and other Christians and people of all faiths. The Second Vatican Council has been described as a 'breath of fresh air blowing through the church'. The Catechism is an attempt to rekindle that inspiration and to remind people of the council's vision of the Church and its role in the world. So many teachings and insights of the council are incorporated in the text.

The essential teachings of the Church do not change, as Christian faith does not change. But they do develop, as does the way of expressing and understanding them. As Pope John Paul II put it, 'the Catechism contains both old and new material because the faith is always the same, yet the source of new light'. The continuity of Church teaching is also underlined in the structure of the new Catechism, which follows the same pattern as the earlier Roman Catechism, the Catechism of the Council of Trent. According to one of the bishops involved in the new Catechism, the wide use of quotations from many ancient sources also helps to emphasize the continuity of the Church's teaching.

Q.3 If this is a 'new' presentation of Catholic teaching, why are there so many quotations and where are they from?

A. The hundreds of quotations in the Catechism, which date back many centuries, help to show the richness and variety of Catholic belief and its continuity and consistency since the start of Christianity 2,000 years ago.

Most of the references and quotations come from the Old and New Testaments. As these are not always given in detail it is important for any reader of the Catechism also to have a Bible to hand. The Catechism uses the RSV and NRSV translations. It is important when considering passages from Scripture to remember that they are used in various ways, not always literally. Sometimes for example, they can be allegorical, with a particular story told to illustrate other events or truths. Thus Moses crossing the Red Sea, leading the Israelites to safety from the Egyptian soldiers, foretells Christ's victory in freeing us from sin and death.

Large numbers of quotations come from church Councils dating back to the first general council at Nicaea, which was summoned in 325 by the first Roman emperor to become a Christian, Constantine. The Council of Trent, called in 1545 to deal with the Reformation, is quoted 99 times and there are also quotations from the catechism produced after that Council. More than twenty Popes down the ages are quoted, and many quotations are taken from the teachings of the present Pope, John Paul II. Other sources included are the Code of Canon Law of the Church, liturgies including those of the Eastern Catholic Rites, and the Roman Missal.

Dozens of saints are quoted. Female saints include Joan of Arc, Teresa of Avila and Catherine of Siena. There are also many quotations from the saints of the Middle Ages, a time when, in spite of the upheaval in religious life, spirituality flourished. The earliest quotation, apart from those from the Bible, comes from one of the first Fathers of the Church, Clement of Rome (first century AD), in his proclamation of Christian belief in redemption by the death of Jesus.

But in case this list suggests that there is much backward looking in the Catechism, the balance is more than redressed by the vast number of quotations from the Second Vatican Council, which of course was the inspiration for it. Among the council documents included are those on liturgical change and reform, the mass media, relations with non-Christians, Christian education, training of priests and updating religious life. Many documents, such as *Familiaris Consortio* and *Sollicitudo Rei Socialis*, were produced after the council, continuing its work and teaching. Selections from several of these are included. The variety is impressive and inspiring.

Q.4 How should the Catechism be read?

A. The Catechism is not a book to be read as one usually reads a book, from page 1 to the final page. This is because it is not written as an ordinary book with a beginning, middle and end but as a reference text which can be consulted according to the reader's requirements and level of knowledge.

Some commentators have suggested that to get the most from this long text, it would be best to start at the end with Part Four, a short and concise section on prayer. This could help the reader to grasp and appreciate the basic aim of the entire Catechism, which is to develop and better understand our relationship with God and the way we can integrate our faith and life. Cardinal Hume said in his pastoral letter to launch the catechism: 'We must read it with the eyes of faith and we will then glimpse something of God and his purpose for our lives.'

To help us to do that and also to explain what it means to listen to God throughout our lives, the section on prayer culminates in the most perfect of prayers, that which Jesus taught us, the Lord's Prayer, or 'Our Father'. It is perhaps not a bad idea to start any reading of the Catechism with a brief prayer to the Holy Spirit to open the 'eyes of faith' for us and to guide our reading. In fact the Catechism reminds us that the Church invites us to call on the Holy Spirit before we take any important action.

Some readers may turn early to Part Three dealing with the Church's basic teaching on moral questions and how this affects daily lives, for example in marriage, at work or in society. But this section really depends upon the vision of human life in relation with God developed in Part One. Here it is important to do two things. First, to read the General Introduction to this section, which goes into detail about how we learn to judge between right and wrong, good and evil, and how this is affected in various degrees by our conscience, passions and habits. It also explains how guilt incurred by wrongdoing can be lessened, and how some actions are judged to be always essentially wrong and against the moral law. These include, for instance, blasphemy, murder, abortion and adultery.

Second, it is important to remember that the Catechism is setting out broad and strict principles that are the basis of Church teaching. It is not attempting to deal with individual actions or circumstances. This will be the task of the local catechisms and other teaching books that will be produced throughout the world. The Catechism is mainly devoted to setting out the laws of the Catholic Church, not their pastoral application.

This book is not easy reading, and some of its teaching may seem difficult. But Cardinal Hume wrote in his pastoral letter: 'I rejoice in the presence of the Holy Spirit at work in the Church guiding in a special manner those with divine authority to teach. I know that if I do not understand at once what is being taught, or find a particular teaching difficult to make my own, I am always right to accept and follow the teaching of the Church. There lies the pathway to salvation.'

Q.5 For whom is the Catechism written?

A. The short answer is that it is written for everybody who is interested in the teaching of the Catholic Church whether they belong to it or not. The Pope writes in his introduction to the Catechism: 'It is offered to every individual who asks us to give an account of the hope that is in us.' It is also addressed to all the faithful who wish to deepen their knowledge and understanding of the 'unfathomable riches of salvation'. We hope it will also help those in other Christian traditions to 'understand the Catholic faith more clearly and affirm the riches of their own tradition'.

However it is important to realize that the Catechism is essentially a reference text addressed to the bishops of the Church because they have the primary responsibility for teaching and explaining the Catholic faith and its application to daily life at all levels. For this reason it is known as a 'major catechism' whereas the Baltimore Catechism, or the little Penny Catechism, produced about a hundred years ago, were called 'minor' because they were written in simple language and were designed for those learning the faith, especially children. (The new Catechism is definitely not intended for children or young people. Its teaching will need to be interpreted and presented in simpler local catechisms specially designed for them.)

Although the text is primarily for bishops, it is hoped that it will also give greater confidence and surety about Catholic doctrine to all involved in teaching the faith, at home, in schools or in parishes. Priests are asked to encourage and guide the use of the Catechism by teachers and catechists. There is increasing emphasis on adult education in the Church today, and the bishops of England and Wales recommend the Catechism for all adults learning about the faith, especially those involved in the Rite of Christian Initiation of Adults. But they point out that it must not be seen as 'a book giving all the answers' or prevent the processes of searching and exploration which are so essential to learning. Recommending the Catechism also to students in seminaries and to Catholic theologians, the bishops hope that it will help to encourage

collaboration between the theologians and those who instruct the
faithful.

Q.6 How does this Catechism present the teaching of the Church? Why is it not in the traditional teaching form of question and answer?

A. In the Catechism, the teaching of the Church is divided into four
separate but closely linked sections with a great many cross-references.
They are not in question and answer form as in the Penny Catechism
or the Baltimore Catechism because the various sections of teaching are
not simple statements or answers to questions, but rather try to express
the teaching of the Church in as complete a way as possible and to
encourage discussion.

The Catechism is not intended to be committed to memory: it is far
too complex for that, although it is suggested that the summaries of the
contents at the end of each chapter are models for the type of teaching
that could be learned by heart.

The body of the Catechism is divided into four main parts. This is
not to suggest that Catholic life can be easily divided into faith and
works but because the teaching of the Church has traditionally been
presented in this way. The sections are: The Creed, The Sacraments,
The Commandments, and Prayer.

Part One, based as it is on the Apostles' Creed, sets out belief in a
Trinitarian God, creator, saviour and sanctifier, in creation, in humanity made in the image of God, in angels, in sin and the devil, in Jesus
the Son of God made man and his mission, in the Holy Spirit's mission
in sanctifying the Church, in redemption, and in life after death. The
emphasis of Part One is on the Trinitarian nature of faith and on the
missions of the Son and the Spirit, the fruit of which is made available
through the whole Church here and in heaven.

Part Two concentrates on the way that we can enjoy and develop
the life that God has intended for us, his children, through the
sacraments.

Part Three deals with faith in action and the moral teaching of the
Church: how we should live if we claim to be followers of Jesus. A great
deal of space is given to the Ten Commandments, the moral law, the
Christian idea of love, and the laws of the Church. This section does

not give all this teaching in detail, but in essence. It is left to the bishops and other teachers in any particular place to develop the teaching in a pastoral way.

Part Four is devoted to the basis of Christian life, our relationship to God in prayer. Looking at the prayer Jesus gave us, the Lord's Prayer, this section analyses what these words teach us about how and why we should pray. The Lord's Prayer was used as a summary of how Christians should relate to God the Father.

Each section is divided into many numbered paragraphs. The subjects are listed in a comprehensive index, which makes it easy for the reader to check the teaching of the Church on any specific topic.

Q.7 Who wrote the Catechism and how far has the Pope been involved?

A. Although this book is designed as a complete and official summary of Roman Catholic teaching, it has not been written in Rome by Vatican staff or by Pope John Paul II. In fact Cardinal Joseph Ratzinger is quoted as saying 'Not a single word was written in Rome'. The Cardinal was of course referring to the main text of the Catechism, not to the introduction, which the Pope did write.

The final version is the work of literally hundreds of minds in the Church. It is truly a 'catholic', that is, universal, book. In this it differs greatly from the Catechism of the Council of Trent, which was mostly written in Rome.

This is how the text of the new Catechism was produced:

1985 At the end of the Extraordinary Synod of bishops called by the Pope in Rome to celebrate the twentieth anniversary of the closing of the Second Vatican Council several bishops, including some from developing countries, where there is a dearth of teaching materials, said they would like to see a new Catechism reflecting the teaching of that Council, which had influenced the Church in so many ways. The call for the new Catechism came originally from the bishops of Korea, Senegal and Mauritius. From the outset it was acknowledged that the new Catechism should be both biblical and liturgical. The proposal was formally put by Cardinal Bernard Law of Boston and the Pope immediately accepted it and agreed that the project should go ahead.

1986 Pope John Paul II appointed a group of twelve cardinals and bishops chaired by Cardinal Ratzinger to prepare a draft of the Catechism. They were helped by an editorial committee of seven diocesan bishops, all experts in theology and teaching the faith. They came from Italy, Spain, France, Chile, Argentina, America and England (Bishop David Konstant of Leeds). Later they were joined by a priest of the Eastern Rite from Lebanon and a co-ordinating secretary, a Dominican theologian. Nine drafts were made.

1989 The third draft was sent to all the bishops of the world.

1990 Their comments and more than 24,000 proposed amendments were sent back to the committee.

1991 Four revisions were carried out and the text substantially amended.

1992 The final text, written in French, was approved by the Pope in June, and published in November.

1993 Translations appeared in all other major European languages except English, where there were problems with inclusive language (e.g. 'humankind', 'human being') and matching the English accurately to the French. Eventually the English translation of the text was revised by Archbishop D'Arcy of Hobart, Tasmania, who removed most of the inclusive language, and replaced it with such terms as 'mankind' and 'man'. He also stuck faithfully to French vocabulary and idiom, even though this results in some strange use of English words, such as the reference, in the passage on the resurrection, to 'concrete men'.

1994 The final translation of the English version was approved by the Vatican and the Catechism was published in the various English-speaking countries including the USA and Canada.

Probably no book has been influenced by so many people and gone through so many detailed revisions. As the Pope says in his introduction, it is a result of the collaboration of the bishops of the whole Church.

Naturally, as head of the Roman Catholic Church, the Pope played an important role in the production of the Catechism. He explains in his introduction that he made the desire for the book 'my own, considering it as fully responding to a real need of the universal Church and of the particular churches'. He declares it 'a sure norm for teaching the faith' and hopes it will serve to renew the Church as it continues its pilgrimage. Although he has not personally written the Catechism, some 137 references to his various teachings and writings are included.

Q.8 Are all parts of the Catechism equally important?

A. In one sense all parts of the Catechism are equally important because they make up one whole and unified presentation of the essential teaching of the Catholic Church. Each part has to be considered in relation to the rest, as the great number of cross-references indicate. The Catholic faith is a complete faith and those who wish to become members of the Church are required to accept all its teaching. It is not an 'à la carte' teaching from which we can pick and choose as we wish. The Church claims that its teaching is true, and truth is not relative as no truth is truer than any other. However, there are two senses in which all the contents of the Catechism are not equally important or essential.

First there is what is known in the Church as the 'hierarchy of truths'. In brief, this means that some truths are more at the heart of Christianity than others. They are the central truths revealed by God from which other truths are developed. They are focal points, essential to Christian faith. They are expressed clearly in the Creed, which starts with the belief in God as creator of all, and continues on to the central teaching of Christianity, that of the Incarnation, God the Son becoming man to offer us all eternal life.

Second, there are also teachings in the Catechism that Catholics are obliged to accept because they have been formally defined as infallible doctrine by the Pope. The word 'infallible' is sometimes misunderstood. (See paragraphs 889–892 in the Catechism.) It does not mean that everything the Pope teaches is without error, or cannot be questioned. He only calls on the gift of infallibility on special and infrequent occasions. The last time an infallible teaching was proclaimed by a Pope was in 1950, when Pius XII defined the dogma that at her death, Mary the Mother of Jesus had been taken up body and soul to be in the presence of God in heaven. This is known as 'The Assumption of the Virgin Mary'. However the Catechism includes many other kinds of teachings and comments from saints, theologians and Popes that are not essential to Catholic teaching and have varying degrees of importance. Passages that are considered to be less important to the argument or that simply serve as illustrations or illuminations of any particular teaching are set in a smaller type face. Some are simply given as footnotes.

Q.9 There have been reports that the Catechism has introduced new sins such as drunken driving, fiddling taxes or expenses or taking drugs. Is this true?

A. Some newspapers ran headlines claiming that new sins are included in the Catechism. They are totally wrong. There is no such thing as new sin. Sin is always sin; it does not change. Wrong can never be right, evil can never be good no matter how good the intention. Injustice can never be justice. Certainly some actions described in the new Catechism as sins were not mentioned in previous catechisms, but this is only because these actions only became possible or were even thought of in recent times. These include such sins as drunken driving, because this endangers human life, and fiddling expenses or legitimate taxes, which are both forms of stealing, forbidden by the seventh commandment. Gambling in moderation is not forbidden. It is only wrong if it becomes excessive, at which stage it can threaten a person's livelihood or family relationships. Our human life does not belong to us. It is given to us by God the creator and we have a duty to look after it and not expose it to unreasonable risks.

To talk about the Catechism 'inventing' new sins is to misunderstand the meaning of sin. Anything that goes against the love of God, our neighbour or ourselves has always been considered sinful by the Church. The Catechism is not trying to spoil or restrict people's lives with formidable lists of sins, rather it is trying to show the way to a fulfilled life free from the unhappiness that sin can bring.

Q.10 What is Vatican II and why is it so often quoted in the Catechism?

A. 'Vatican II' is the generally-used shorthand for the Second Vatican Ecumenical Council of the Roman Catholic Church, held in Rome between 1962 and 1965, to renew the Church and guide it into the modern age.

An Ecumenical Council is an assembly of the world's bishops, called or at least approved by the Pope as part of the solemn Magisterium or teaching office of the Church. 'Ecumenical' is derived from a Greek word, originally meaning 'under one roof', but now used to express universality.

Complex as they are to arrange and to carry out, Ecumenical Councils do not take place very often. In the whole history of the Church there have only been twenty-one. The first was in Nicaea in 325. The twentieth was Vatican I (1869–70), and the twenty-first, Vatican II, was the first to be held in almost a hundred years.

Vatican II was called by Pope John XXIII. Its aims were to bring up to date (the Italian word is *aggiornamento*) the laws and practices of the Church, and make its theology more relevant and dynamic, ready to face the great problems of the contemporary world. Pope John presided over the preparatory commissions, whose enormous task it was to arrange the agenda, and he supervised the first session of the Council up to its solemn closing on 8 December 1962.

By the time the Second Session opened on 29 September the following year, Pope John had died and had been succeeded by Pope Paul VI who, in his opening address, reaffirmed the Council's purpose 'to open up new horizons in the Church, and to tap the fresh spring water of the doctrine and grace of Christ Our Lord and let it flow over the earth'.

The Second Vatican Council produced a total of sixteen documents of Church teaching including topics as diverse as art or Abraham on the one hand, and worship and youth on the other.

The full list is impressive. The first, issued on 4 December 1963, was the Constitution on the Sacred Liturgy. This was arguably the document which had the most immediate and dramatic effect on the faithful, laying the foundations for the vernacular celebration of Mass, which for centuries had always been said in Latin throughout the world. The scope of the Council was far wider, as the list of its documents shows. The Constitution on the Liturgy was followed by a Decree on Mass Media, then the Dogmatic Constitution on the Church, the Decrees on the Eastern Rite Churches, on Ecumenism, on the Office of Bishops (which had important things to say on the way they share responsibility for the whole Church, not just for their own dioceses). Then followed Decrees on Religious Life, the Training of Clergy, the Declaration on

Christian Education and on Non-Christian Religions, the Dogmatic Constitution on Divine Revelation, a Decree on the Apostolate of Lay People, a Declaration on Religious Liberty, the Decrees on the Church's Missionary Activity, and on the Ministry and Life of Priests and, finally, the Pastoral Constitution on the Church in the Modern World, which is widely quoted in the Catechism under its Latin name, *Gaudium et Spes*, that is, 'Joy and Hope'.

The spirit of Vatican II inspired the Catechism, which contains and builds on many of its insights. Little wonder, then, that the Council is so often quoted in the text and the footnotes.

PART ONE

THE PROFESSION OF FAITH

Q.11 What does the Catechism say about the purpose of human life?

A. Addressing this most fundamental of questions at the start, the Catechism explains that God has made each human being for himself and to share his own blessed life. Our purpose is to seek God, know him and love him with all our strength. As the Acts of the Apostles states, 'In him we live and move and have our being' (Acts 17:28). (54)

Perhaps one of the best known quotations on this subject, included in the Catechism, comes from St Augustine: 'Our hearts are restless until they rest in you.'

Throughout history people have expressed their relationship with God through sacrifices, prayers and rituals. They have shown that we are essentially religious beings. The Catechism points out that all religions are based on this constant human search for God. (28)

This desire for God is written on each human heart and only in God will the heart find true happiness. As Vatican II taught: 'For if man exists it is because God has created him through love, and through love continues to hold him in existence. He cannot live fully according to the truth unless he freely acknowledges that love and entrusts himself to the creator.' It is because of his great love for each of us that God desires us all to be saved and share in eternal life. To achieve this he sent his only Son, Jesus Christ. Through him we are the adopted children of God himself.

So that this message might reach throughout the world, Christ instructed his apostles to go and preach to all nations, baptizing them in the name of the Blessed Trinity. Those who have received this good news are also responsible for spreading it as far as possible, and for handing it on to future generations.

However, although each human being is made for God we can forget or even reject him. This can be because of the evil in our world, ignorance of religious teaching, bad example from those calling themselves Christians or simply the many cares of life. There are also those who because of sin try to hide from God and ignore his call. But no matter how hard we may try to escape from God and ignore him, he never ceases to call us to him and his life of love and happiness.

For our part we must make every effort to find God through our intellect, 'upright heart' and the example of those who do believe. (30)

Q.12 What is meant by 'God'?

A. This is *the* question of questions. People have been asking it since the dawn of history. And there is no simple answer to it. The Catechism tackles it in two sections (199ff. and 279ff.). Its starting-point is the incident, recounted in the book of Exodus, chapter 3, of Moses and the burning bush. The Lord, God, appeared to Moses in the desert in the form of a burning bush. Moses asked God directly our question: 'Who are you?' God replied: 'I AM WHO AM'. In Hebrew, 'I am who am' is both a name and a verb. It is written YHWH and pronounced *Yahweh*. (213)

Both the Christian Creeds (the Apostles' and the Nicene) begin with the words 'I (or We) believe in (one) God', and straight away describe just two of his many attributes: he is Father and he is almighty.

Many religions call God 'Father' because he is the creator of everything. Jesus told his followers to do so, but in a previously unheard-of way, when he taught them the 'Our Father'.

Although we normally refer to God as 'he', God, as spirit, transcends human distinction between genders, is neither male nor female but both Father and Mother.

As almighty, God is understood as being able to do all things. 'Without him was made nothing that was made', as the Creed says. He is the one and only *necessary* being. All other beings are, to use the technical word, *contingent*, that is to say, they do not *have* to exist. God alone, since he is Being, cannot *not* exist. He is the beginning and end of all else that exists.

Theologians, philosophers and saints have devoted themselves, over the centuries, to working out the almost inexhaustible meaning of the word 'God' and have gone on to describe him as perfect truth and perfect love. In all of this, of course, humans are restricted to human ideas and human language, from which it follows that all our efforts to express God will be inadequate.

Nevertheless, much of civilized thought, art and literature would be incomparably impoverished if human beings in the light of their faith had not dared, in so far as they could, to express what the idea of God meant to them and their generations. In its most profound sense, Christians say with St John 'God is love'.

God, however, did not leave us entirely to our own devices. He gradually revealed himself to us, and as a result we also know that God is both one and three: one God, yet three Divine Persons, each distinct from the other. These three we know as the Father, the Son and the Holy Spirit, or the Blessed Trinity. In an effort to distinguish one from the other, we see the Father as the creator of all things from nothing, the Son as the redeemer of the human race, and the Holy Spirit as the sanctifier and sustainer of all that is, and also the 'soul' of the Church. (238ff., 797, 813)

The clearest image of God that has been given to us is in the person of Jesus Christ, God become man. Further, Christians believe that every human person is created, as the book of Genesis says, in the image of God. This said, we cannot claim to have exhausted our question. However, in a sense, all that follows in this book and, indeed, in the Catechism itself will help to fill out our knowledge of who and what God is and what his love for us means for us all.

Q.13 How can we come to know God?

A. We come to know and to believe in God only because he has chosen to reveal himself to us. He does this in many ways, not least by giving us human intelligence which we use to interpret what we see of creation around us and so we are able to arrive, not without difficulty, at the conclusion that he exists. (31ff.)

However, apart from this, God has, in the course of human history, revealed himself by interaction with the human beings he created, for example, Abraham, and ultimately, in the mystery of the Incarnation, he came to live among us in the person of his Son, made man, Jesus Christ.

The books of the Jewish Scriptures, the Old Testament, tell in many well-known and loved stories how God, despite the persistent infidelities of his people, renewed his covenant with them (repeatedly expressed in the words 'I will be your God and you will be my people') and guided them through the words of his spokespersons: the patriarchs, judges, prophets, the apostles and their successors, to find their destiny with him. The process began with the covenant he made with Noah after the flood. Then followed a succession of great patriarchs: Abraham, 'our father in faith', who, having affirmed his faith in the one God, was given the responsibility of fathering the new nation, the People of God; Isaac, Jacob and Joseph followed, then later Moses and his brother Aaron who led the people out of captivity in Egypt to find their destiny in the Promised Land.

Many holy women played significant roles also in the history of the covenant. Among them were Sarah, the wife of Abraham, Rebecca, Judith, Esther and, of course, Mary who was to become the mother of Jesus.

In Jesus, God established the new and eternal covenant, binding divinity and humanity together in one eternal act of love and self-giving, the full significance of which we may only realize when our life on this earth has ended and we arrive, hopefully, at the fullness of divine revelation.

In the meantime, however, we find hope and divine revelation both in word and writings; tradition and sacred Scripture, and the teaching of the Church, which was commanded by Jesus to bring the good news of salvation to the ends of the earth. In this way the eternal truths are handed on from generation to generation and, as a result, we grow in faith and in the life of the Spirit. (80ff.)

Q.14 What is tradition?

A. The Church teaches that the word of God was entrusted to the apostles by Christ the Lord and the Holy Spirit. Although much of what we believe to be God's word is contained in the Scriptures, nevertheless the Holy Spirit's inspiration is not limited to the Bible. So the successors to the apostles, that is the Pope and the bishops in communion with him, enlightened by the Spirit of Truth, are given the mission to explain and spread the word of God in its entirety.

That there is a continuous, living tradition in the Church is illustrated dramatically when we realize that the first generation of Christians did not have any written account of the teachings of Jesus. Their knowledge and understanding of these were initially handed on by word of mouth. These same teachings were eventually written down during the first century, as what we now call the New Testament. The production of these writings demonstrates the process of living tradition. It was the Holy Spirit, working in and through the early Church, who inspired the writers of the gospels, epistles and Acts of the Apostles. (105ff.)

The Catechism quotes Vatican II's teaching that the apostles entrusted the 'sacred deposit' of the faith (the *depositum fidei*), contained in sacred Scripture and tradition, to the whole Church. The task of authentically interpreting the word of God, whether written or in oral tradition, has been entrusted to the living teaching office of the Church alone. Its teaching authority is exercised in the name of Jesus Christ by the bishops in communion with the successor of St Peter, the Pope, the Bishop of Rome. This teaching authority of the Church is known as the Magisterium. It is not, of course, superior to the word of God, but is its servant. (175, 84, 85ff.)

Through the assistance of the Holy Spirit, knowledge and understanding of the whole heritage of faith develop and grow in the life of the Church. In this way too, the whole Church is protected from error when, 'from the bishops to the last of the faithful', it accepts and expresses universal consent in matters of faith and morals (Vatican II).

Q.15 What is the Bible?

A. The Bible is probably the most widely read book in the world. There are about two thousand million copies in circulation with a further two million added every year.

The Bible began, about 5,000 years before Christ, as little more than a few inscribed clay or stone tablets which, together with a great body of folklore and camp-fire tales, told of a God who revealed himself to human beings in the course of history.

Despite appearances, the Bible is not a single book; it is a collection of 73 writings, books, articles, letters, poems, and psalms, or praise-songs, composed, written down and collected over the course of centuries. The Church teaches that God the Holy Spirit inspired the human writers of the Bible texts so that their words were both their own work and the word of God. (109, 110)

Christians recognize two main groups of these writings; those before Christ, which are known to Christians as the Old Testament, and those after, largely about Christ and his teachings, and the life of the early

Christian communities, the New Testament. This is made up of some eyewitness accounts of Jesus' life and teachings, together with other documents, such as the letters of St Paul, which were written to guide and instruct the first Christians. We know about the life and teaching of Jesus from the four gospels (called the Gospels according to Matthew, Mark, Luke and John). In the days after Jesus' ascension these were passed on by word of mouth and later put together in written form. They wrote, as St John says, 'so that you may believe that Jesus is the Christ, the Son of God, and that believing you may have life in his name' (John 20:31).

The Old Testament is read by Christians in the light of their belief in Christ crucified and risen. It is he who is the centre of salvation history, and all that happened before and since refers to him. (112, 128)

The Bible is an invaluable source of wisdom and devotion. From it we take most of the texts which now go to make up the Christian liturgy. It is 'the very soul of sacred theology'. The Catechism quotes Hugh of Saint-Victor: 'All Sacred Scripture is but one book, and that one book is Christ, because all divine Scripture speaks of Christ and all divine Scripture is fulfilled in Christ.' (134)

Q.16 What is faith and how should it affect our daily lives?

A. Faith is, first and foremost, a gift from God, which enables us to know that he exists. Through this gift we are able to accept God's grace and to respond to it in the act of faith, 'I believe', and put our trust in him. (153)

Faith is above reason but not contrary to it. The Church teaches that we can, by the use of our reason, recognize in the created universe natural indications of God's existence, and arrive at the point where faith is possible. The grace of the Holy Spirit builds on these signs and enables us to make an act of supernatural faith in the creator and all that he has revealed to us. Properly understood, the truth of faith is not in conflict with the truths of human science. (156, 159)

God is Truth. When he has revealed himself to us and we, in turn, have come to know him, our lives cannot be the same again. At once our intellect and free will are challenged to submit freely to his word. This is called the obedience of faith. Mary the Mother of Jesus is seen as the perfect model of faithful obedience in her *fiat*, Latin for 'Let it be so', at the Annunciation.

Being a spiritual gift, faith cannot be 'seen'. It can however be recognized in the way that those who have received the gift live their lives in accordance with the teachings of Jesus. Pope John Paul II in his prologue to the Catechism says: 'If faith is not expressed in works, it is dead (cf. James 2:14–16) and cannot bear fruit unto eternal life.'

For the Christian, faith in God cannot be separated from belief in the one whom he has sent – Jesus Christ his only Son. 'No one can say "Jesus is Lord" except by the Holy Spirit' (1 Cor 12:3). When St Peter declared Jesus to be the Christ, the Son of the living God, Jesus said to him: 'Blessed are you, Peter, for flesh and blood has not revealed this to you, but my Father who is in heaven' (Matt 16:17).

The truths of the Christian faith are summed up in the great traditional Creeds (a word which comes from the Latin *credo*, I believe), the Nicene Creed, commonly understood to date back to the Council of Nicaea in 325, although it may be a version of an even earlier creed, and the Apostles' Creed, which dates from about AD 500, but which is popularly attributed to the apostles in its origins. Of the two, the Apostles' Creed is the shorter, the Nicene is more explicit and detailed.

Faith is a shared experience, a shared gift and something to be celebrated liturgically. The Christian will often find him or herself reciting the Creed publicly as part of a service of worship. This is in itself a grace-filled act and serves, not just to remind us of the truths which it contains, but also to increase the very grace of faith which it celebrates. (168)

It is, unfortunately, possible to lose our faith by rejecting what we know to be right. To prevent this, as the Catechism says, we must nourish it with the word of God; we must beg the Lord, in prayer, to increase our faith.

Q.17 What are the Creeds?

A. A creed (from the Latin *credo*, 'I believe') is the name given to a brief and authoritative formulation of the essential elements of the Christian faith. Although there have been many formulations of the faith over the centuries, expressing it in many different ways, two hold a special place in the life of the Church; the Apostles' Creed, so called because it is taken to summarize the faith as preached by the apostles, and the Nicene Creed, named after the Ecumenical Council held in Nicaea in the year 325, which was called to draw up a clear statement of the faith, although the Creed did not reach its final form until the Council of Constantinople in 381. This Creed is largely shared by Churches of both East and West. (195)

The Apostles' Creed.

I believe in God the Father almighty,
creator of heaven and earth.
I believe in Jesus Christ, his only Son, our Lord.
He was conceived by the power of the Holy Spirit
and born of the Virgin Mary.
He suffered under Pontius Pilate,
was crucified, died and was buried.
He descended to the dead.
On the third day he rose again.
He ascended into heaven
and is seated at the right hand of the Father.
He will come again to judge the living and the dead.
I believe in the Holy Spirit,
the holy catholic Church,
the Communion of Saints,
the forgiveness of sins,
the resurrection of the body, and the life everlasting. Amen.

The Nicene Creed.

We believe in one God,
the Father, the Almighty,
maker of heaven and earth
and of all that is, seen and unseen.
We believe in one Lord, Jesus Christ,
the only Son of God,
eternally begotten of the Father,
God from God, Light from Light,
true God from true God,
begotten, not made,
of one being with the Father.
Through him all things were made.
For us men and for our salvation, he came down from heaven:

by the power of the Holy Spirit
he became incarnate of the Virgin Mary, and became man.
For our sake he was crucified under Pontius Pilate;
he suffered death and was buried.
On the third day he rose again in accordance with the Scriptures;
he ascended into heaven and is seated at the right hand of the
     Father.
He will come again in glory to judge the living and the dead,
and his kingdom will have no end.
We believe in the Holy Spirit, the Lord, the giver of life,
who proceeds from the Father and the Son.
With the Father and the Son he is worshipped and glorified.
He has spoken through the prophets.
We believe in one holy catholic and apostolic Church.
We acknowledge one baptism for the forgiveness of sins.
We look for the resurrection of the dead,
and the life of the world to come. Amen.

The contents of the Creeds form the basis of Part One of the Catechism, on which the questions that follow are based. (487)

Q.18 Why do Christians pray 'In the name of the Father, and of the Son, and of the Holy Spirit'?

A. All Christians are baptized in the name of the Father, Son and Holy Spirit, because this is how God has revealed himself to us. God is Trinity: three divine persons in one Godhead. The mystery of the Holy Trinity is the central mystery of the Christian faith. Jesus revealed to his disciples the fatherhood of God, his own relationship to the Father and his Son, and the Holy Spirit whom he promised to send into the world to guide and comfort the Church always.

The Father revealed himself to the Israelites of old, who addressed him as 'Father' because they recognized him as their creator and because, in his covenant (that is his agreement with them), he gave himself to them as their protector and guide. (238f.)

Jesus is a further revelation of God's fatherhood, insofar as the Father is the eternal Father of the Son who, in turn, is eternally his Son. Jesus, the Son, further reveals to us the divinity of the Holy Spirit, who co-exists with him and the Father from all eternity and who is sent by the Father and the Son into our world to guide us in the truth. Although there had been suggestions or traces of his Trinitarian being in the early Hebrew writings, the Old Testament, it is only in Jesus, the Second Person made man, that the Blessed Trinity is fully revealed. (237)

Over the centuries, especially in the early years of the Church, much theological time was spent in the study of the mystery of the Trinity. God is not *three Gods*, he is one. Father, Son and Spirit are not just three names of God, or ways of considering him; they are three distinct and equal persons. And yet in those three persons there is but one God. How God can be both three and one at the same time is, of course, the great mystery. We shall only come close to understanding it when, with God's grace, we share the beatific vision in the life to come. (236, 248, 251, 256, 260)

Q.19 The Creed calls God 'almighty'. What does this mean? How does it square with his apparent inability to prevent illness, suffering and other evils?

A. We call God 'almighty' in the Creed because we believe that, as creator of all that is, he has complete power over the entire universe, which operates according to his eternal laws. He is also Lord of all history, guiding the hearts and wills of men and women, through his grace, so that their lives, and thus the course of history, develop in keeping with his overall plan, or fail to do so, as the case may be. Human history is a complex tapestry of success and failure, good and evil. The good is willed by God; the evil he tolerates as a result of his gift of free will to his creation. The Catechism does admit that, in some cases, God *seems* to be powerless in the face of evil. At times evil certainly seems to triumph, at least in the short run. We are face-to-face with a mystery here. This is shown at its most dramatic in the suffering and death of the Son of God. But in the resurrection of that same Son, God overcomes evil. The Catechism quotes St Paul's first letter to the Corinthians: Christ crucified is 'the power of God and the Wisdom of God. For the foolishness of God is wiser than men, and the weakness of God is stronger than men' (1 Cor 1:24–25). (272ff.)

The greatest evil of all, of course, is sin, which offends God himself.

Yet we know that there is no sin so great that God is not prepared to forgive it. In forgiving sin God does, indeed, overcome evil by the power of his almighty love. Much suffering is caused because of our fallen nature and our refusal at times to live in accordance with the basic law to love God and our neighbours as ourselves.

In the physical universe things exist in movement. They appear and disappear, and in between, they develop, grow to perfection and then decline. Thus the whole of creation is on a journey to its ultimate perfection. Until that perfection is achieved, and because there is physical good in the world, there will also be physical evil. But just as the moral evil of sin is overcome by the love of God, so also the other evils in the universe will disappear in the long run. Again, quoting St Paul, the Catechism says: 'We know that in everything God works for good for those who love him' (Rom 8:28). (268f., 309ff.)

Q.20 What is meant by 'unseen' creation?

A. The unseen world is that part of creation which we call the spirit world. Sacred Scripture speaks of spiritual, non-bodily beings, called angels, and both Scripture and tradition are constant in their teaching that angels exist. The word 'angel' comes from the Greek word for a messenger. (328ff.)

Pope Pius XII spoke of angels as 'personal and immortal creatures, surpassing in perfection all visible creatures'. Interestingly, and despite that description of them, although angels are considered a 'higher' kind of being than humans, nevertheless, nowhere in Scripture or tradition are they described, as humans are, as 'made in God's likeness'.

Throughout the Scriptures the angels are shown as messengers from God to people and (sometimes) vice versa. They closed Eden to the first parents, gave guidance and protection to many of the patriarchs and prophets, and eventually brought the good news of the Incarnation to Mary and comforted her Son in his agony on Mount Olivet. Angels are described at the tomb of Jesus on the first Easter morning. They sent the apostles back to Jerusalem after the Ascension: 'Why do you stand here, looking up to heaven?'

For the Church, too, the angels are ever present; they are invoked in the liturgy of the Eucharist and in the Funeral Service, and holy tradition says that each of us is constantly guided and protected by a personal guardian angel. At the end of the world, when all will be renewed, we are destined to join the heavenly choir of angels in the eternal praise of God. (328ff., 335)

Q.21 What is the devil?

A. The presence of evil in a universe created by an all-good God will always be a problem, even though philosophers and other scholars claim that the very existence of good makes evil a possibility. That is to say, where 'good' exists there must at least be the possibility of 'non-good', i.e. evil. Both Scripture and tradition, however, speak of evil, not just as a philosophical principle but as embodied in an individual, 'Satan' or 'the devil': an angelic being of pure spirit, created by God as good, but who freely and definitively rejected God and thus became the source of evil in the world. However, he is only a creature. His power is not infinite. Although he may well cause serious harm in our spiritual life, he cannot prevent the coming of God's Kingdom. (391, 414)

The book of Genesis portrays Satan as the instigator of humanity's original sin of disobedience when he tempted the first parents, Adam and Eve, to defy God and eat of the fruit of the tree of knowledge of good and evil.

Jesus himself spoke of Satan, whom he called 'a murderer from the beginning' (John 8:44), and the gospels show that Jesus, although he was the Son of God, did not escape the temptations of the devil. Before he began his public preaching, Jesus went into the desert to pray. He remained there for forty days and nights, during which time the devil tempted him to commit sins of pride and self-interest. (538–540)

Similarly, the devil is understood to be constantly on the watch to tempt us in accordance with our weaknesses. The first epistle of St Peter (3:8–9) says: 'Be sober and watchful, for the devil, like a roaring lion, prowls around, seeking whom he may devour. Resist him, firm in your faith.' The Church also teaches that we are never helpless victims of temptation. The grace of God is always available to those who want to ask for it. (2847)

Q.22 How do humans differ from the rest of creation?

A. The Bible tells us that God created us, male and female, 'in his own likeness'. Humans, which are both spiritual and bodily beings, are placed on earth as stewards of creation. They are charged with its conservation and development, but they are invited to do this freely. All other earthly creatures, animate or inanimate, follow the physical laws of nature or their instincts without having the freedom to choose what they do. (369, 373)

In the whole of the material world there is no other creature which has the gift of free will. It is the capacity to choose; to love or not to love, to accept freely the law of God or to disobey it. Human beings are therefore unique in all creation. (396)

It is this gift of free will that made original sin possible. Our first parents, in consenting to the suggestions of the devil, abused their freedom and disobeyed God's prohibition. Their sin was, therefore, a sin of both disobedience and pride. (398)

The results were tragic; those who were destined to be God's friends now become afraid of him. The original harmony of creation is broken. Visible creation becomes hostile; human life will now be a struggle, both moral and physical. 'In the sweat of thy brow shalt thou eat bread', God tells Adam. Because of that first act of disobedience, sin becomes a constant factor in human history. (400)

Since we understand Adam and Eve as representing the whole of humanity, all are tainted by, and share in the guilt of their sin, which is known as original sin. Therefore all human beings are deprived of that original holiness for which they were created. We are now all capable of personal sins. And it is our need to be rescued from this situation that is the foundation of the mystery of the redemptive death and resurrection of Jesus. Even at the point of the first sin, our first parents were promised redemption by God. And in the liturgy of Easter Night Christians sing 'O happy fault [original sin] . . . which gained for us so great a Redeemer'. (412)

Q.23 Who is Jesus Christ?

A. Christians believe that the man Jesus of Nazareth was a Jew, born to a young Israelite woman called Miriam, or Mary, in the town known

32 ANSWERS TO QUESTIONS ON THE CATECHISM

to this day as Bethlehem, at the time of King Herod the Great and
Caesar Augustus, the Roman emperor, some 2,000 years ago. A carpenter by trade, Jesus worked alongside St Joseph, Mary's husband, in his
home town of Nazareth. At about the age of thirty he became an
itinerant preacher, gathering about him a band of followers, many of
them fishermen, on the shores of Lake Galilee. Three years later he was
executed as a criminal in Jerusalem under Pontius Pilate, the Roman
governor, in the reign of the emperor Tiberius. Christians believe that
on the third day after his death Jesus rose from the dead, to be alive
again. Forty days later, his followers saw him ascend to heaven to be 'at
the right hand of the Father'. Ever since, he has been proclaimed as the
eternal Son of God made man. (423)

For our knowledge of Jesus we rely mainly on the four gospels, which
are not biographies, although they do contain some details of his life.
They were written primarily as accounts of his teaching, which centred
on his Father's Kingdom of justice and peace, based on love of God and
neighbour. His teaching was delivered in the characteristic style of the
rabbis, in parables: short stories, usually with a 'sting in the tail', which
encouraged his listeners to form their own conclusions and apply his
teaching to their own lives.

There is no doubt that Jesus of Nazareth existed. He was a real human
being, living, working and dying at a given time and in a definite place.
In this very human life he shared the fate of all humanity except the
disaster of personal sin. However, it is in his teachings and in the
extraordinary events that followed his death on a cross that we find that
redeemer who was promised to the first parents even as they were
expelled from Paradise: the one who would save them and their descen-
dants from their sins.

The great mystery of redemption was brought about by the death
and resurrection of Jesus. His teachings about God's Kingdom and the
good news of salvation are the key to our existence. This message was
taken up by the apostles at the Jewish feast of Pentecost when the
Holy Spirit inspired and emboldened them to preach the risen Christ.
It is continued today in the preaching and ministry of the Church.
(425)

The name Jesus (Joshua, in Hebrew) means 'saviour'. At the Annunciation, the Angel Gabriel told Mary to give her son this name because
'he would save his people from their sins' (Matt 1:21). St Luke, in the
Acts of the Apostles, proclaims that 'there is no other name . . . by which

we must be saved' (Acts 4:12), and all Christian liturgical prayer is made 'through Jesus Christ, Our Lord'. (430)

The title 'Christ' is originally Greek and signifies someone who has been anointed or consecrated, a sacred act that was done by the pouring of holy oil. By his very coming into the world, Jesus was consecrated to the service of his Father and all humanity who, through him, become the redeemed children of the Father. (436, 442ff.)

Q.24 What does the word 'incarnation' mean? Why did it take place?

A. St John, in his Gospel, tells us: 'The Word was made flesh and dwelt among us' (1:14). 'Word' here is a translation of the Greek *Logos*, which is the name given to God the Son, the eternal Second Person of the Trinity. He is the Word, that is the expression of the Divine Being. This is the central mystery of Christianity: God the Son, the Second Person of the Blessed Trinity, assumed human nature and became man, without ceasing to be God. That man we know as Jesus of Nazareth. (463)

Was it necessary for God to become man in order to save us? Theoretically, no; a single movement of the divine will would have been enough. So why did the Incarnation take place? It happened so that there would be, in the man, Jesus, a being in whom humanity and divinity could be united as in no other way. Because he became one of us, we can become one with him and with the Father and the Holy Spirit. He became man in order to reconcile us with the Father, to show us the depth and extent of his love and to make it possible for us to 'become partakers of the divine nature' as brothers and sisters of Christ. (457, 458)

In the struggle to understand this great mystery, the Church, especially in the early years, had to wrestle with various heretical theories which tried to explain the Incarnation by denying either the true divinity or the true humanity of Jesus. But the truth, proclaimed universally by the Church, is that Jesus is inseparably true God and true man. He had a human body and a human soul like every person. He was like us in all things, except sin. (464ff.)

In his human person, therefore, Jesus had to learn from his experiences, just like any other human child. In his human will, too, he was subject to and chose to obey the divine will of his Father. He came, as he said, 'to do the will of him who sent me' (John 4:34). (472)

That will, of course, was to achieve the salvation of all humanity, which he did with all the love of which a human heart is capable. As the gospels teach us, there is no greater love than to lay down one's life for one's friends. This is why, in popular devotion, the image of the Sacred Heart is revered as a symbol of the saving love of Jesus. (478)

Q.25 What is the Virgin Birth? Why is it important? Do Catholics worship the Virgin Mary?

A. The Church has traditionally taught that Jesus was conceived in the womb of the Virgin, by the power of God the Holy Spirit, without the involvement of any man, and without her virginity being in any way affected. In order that a worthy mother would be available to bear his Son, God, from all eternity, chose the girl Mary of Nazareth, filling her, from the moment she was conceived, with the fullness of divine grace. Thus she was protected from any taint of original sin or its consequences. (It is her sinlessness that was celebrated in 1854, when Pope Pius IX proclaimed the infallible dogma of her Immaculate Conception, a title that is sometimes mistakenly thought to concern her own virginal conception of Jesus.) (487, 491ff.)

Because of her perfect goodness, Mary was enabled to give her full yet totally free consent to the conception of her Son upon the invitation of the Angel Gabriel at the Annunciation. The Catechism points out that the mysterious manner of Jesus' conception 'surpasses all human understanding and possibility'. It will always remain a mystery for us. (497)

Mary's virginal motherhood is a direct result of the exercise of God's fatherhood. In this way both Jesus' divinity and his humanity are guaranteed. Mary is honoured, therefore, not just as the mother of the man, Jesus, but as truly the Mother of God. It is precisely because she is the Mother of God, and therefore in a unique relationship with the Divinity, that Catholics honour Mary in a special way. They do not offer her the adoration which is due to God alone, but they do honour her as one who in life and death is united with God through her son, in a way that will never be possible for any other human being. As a result, she is called upon as the great intercessor for us with the Godhead, through her son. (971)

Throughout the centuries, some of the greatest works of art and music have been inspired by the Blessed Virgin, including settings of the *Ave Maria*, 'Hail Mary', that ancient prayer beloved of generations of Catholics. (484ff.)

Q.26 How and what did Jesus teach?

A. Both in the way he lived, as well as in his formal preaching and teaching, Jesus was constantly proclaiming the good news of salvation and the love of God. The gospels show him born in the poverty of a stable, a mere shed for animals. The event was proclaimed both to the humble shepherds and to the great and wise Magi. He was subject to the Jewish religious law of circumcision, spent some time as a refugee with Mary and Joseph in Egypt, and upon the family's return lived the life of a normal Jewish youth in Nazareth, their home town, where he worked as a carpenter. At the age of about thirty he began a short period of public teaching as an itinerant rabbi, a word which simply means 'teacher'. His first public appearance was at the bank of the Jordan where his cousin, John the Baptist, was preaching a baptism of repentance, urging all and sundry to confess their sins, turn back to God and be symbolically washed clean in the river. Jesus, although sinless, joined the ranks of pilgrims, and when John protested that he should not submit to baptism, but rather that he, John, should be baptized by Jesus, he insisted on undergoing the ceremony, probably as a sign of his solidarity with ordinary people. (525ff., 535ff.)

Then followed forty days' retreat in the desert, during which Jesus was violently tempted by the devil and comforted and strengthened by angels. After this he began his mission. Coming to the shore of the Sea of Galilee, he made his home at Capernaum, and gathered a group of twelve men, mainly local fishermen, their wives and families, about him and began to teach them of the Kingdom of God and how it was to be established on earth. In summary, everything was to be done for love of God and of our neighbour. His teachings were notable for the authority with which he spoke (unlike, as people said, the Scribes and Pharisees), and for the wonderful signs, most notably healings, that accompanied them. As he said himself, the blind saw, the dumb spoke and the poor had the good news preached to them. His whole public life was spent helping others, particularly those who were outcasts of society, sinners, lepers, prostitutes, to such an extent that, at times, his friends had to urge him to take a break so that he could have some food and rest away from the crowds. (538ff.)

Occasionally he went alone into the desert or onto a mountain to spend time in prayer to his Father. After one such period his disciples asked him to teach them how to pray. In answer, he taught them the prayer we know as the Lord's Prayer, which is used to this day by Christians throughout the world. (2759ff.)

About three years after the beginning of his public life, Jesus and his disciples visited the holy city of Jerusalem for the religious festival of Passover. He celebrated a festive supper with them, during which, by taking on the role of a servant and kneeling to wash their feet, he taught them the fundamental lesson: that to be his followers they must first and foremost be at the service of others. Then, taking the bread and wine of the paschal meal, he instructed them in the celebration of the Eucharist, by means of which they, and millions who came after them, would remember him and assure his presence amongst them to the end of time.

Some of the religious authorities, who resented his teaching, his popularity, and the company he kept, arranged to have him trapped, subjected to a show trial, tortured and executed. This was on the basis of the false accusation both that he 'stirred up the people' to revolution and that he had committed the crime of blasphemy which, in Jewish law, was punished by the death penalty. (595ff.)

So the life of Jesus was brought to an ignominious end on the cross at Golgotha. Evil seemed to triumph. No one suspected what an amazing turn events were to take on the following Sunday with the discovery of his empty tomb. (613ff.)

Q.27 Why did Christ have to suffer the death of a criminal?

A. It is certain that Jesus would have had to die at some time; he was a real human being and therefore subject to the laws of mortality. The tragedy is not that he died, but that his death was at such an early age and was brought about through treachery and injustice.

In the course of his preaching, Jesus challenged many of the accepted, formal attitudes to religion and the religious life, particularly as taught by some of the Scribes, Pharisees and other religious leaders. He also taught with authority. He ate and drank with sinners, applied the laws of God with compassion, and even went as far as to claim to be able to forgive sins, in which many saw an act of blasphemy. Gradually, throughout the years of his public life, the antagonism between Jesus and the religious authorities increased. They began to see him as a threat to their own standing in society. The numbers of his followers continued to grow until, as some saw it, he began to pose problems as a popular, and thus possible, political leader: an intolerable situation for them.

Because the Roman occupiers of the land had taken away the right to exercise the death penalty from the Sanhedrin, the latter handed Jesus over to the Roman Procurator, Pilate, to have him executed as a preacher of sedition.

Could not his Father in some way have prevented such a tragic perversion of justice? Possibly so in theory, but there was a certain inevitability about the manner of Christ's death. On Olivet the night before he died he asked his Father 'If possible, let this chalice pass from me. Nevertheless, not my will but thine be done.'

In doing the will of his Father, in preaching the Kingdom of God as he did, Jesus was the embodiment of all goodness. His very presence and his goodness were in themselves a challenge to those who met him. This challenge could only be met in one of two ways: conversion of heart for those who would accept him, or antagonism on the part of those who were unwilling to do so. In a word, where absolute goodness and truth come face to face with obstinate evil you have the ingredients for a destructive collision. In Jesus' case, that destructive collision took place on Calvary. In being wholly human, Jesus accepted the inevitable human consequences of his words and deeds. Yet good was not defeated, but, in the resurrection, triumphed. (571ff., 599ff., 612)

Q.28 Do Catholics still blame the Jews for the death of Jesus?

A. There has been a shameful thread of anti-Semitism running through much of Christian history, sometimes virulent, and at other times almost invisible or latent. Where anti-Semitism appeared, it was often 'justified' by blaming the Jews, as a race, for the unjust execution of Jesus. This in itself was, of course, a grave injustice and was often no more than a convenient cover-up for other motives, such as jealousy or greed on the part of Christians.

The circumstances surrounding the accusation, trial and death of Jesus, as we read them in the gospels, were complex in the extreme. Personal vendetta, jealousy, pride, ambition, fear and crowd manipulation all played their part. Only God is in a position to allocate blame where it is due. It is for us only to marvel at a mystery so profound and to thank God that out of such a web of evil the redemption of the human race and the forgiveness of our sins was brought about.

So, the short answer to our question is: No. Catholics today do not and should not blame the Jews for the death of Jesus. Insofar as any human blame is to be allocated, it falls on us all since we are sinners and so, in the words of the Catechism, we are all 'authors of Christ's passion'. (A historic Church document, in preparation as the Catechism was published, accepts responsibility for, and asks forgiveness for, the history of anti-Semitism. It is good that the record should be set straight, even at such a late stage in the history of Christianity.) (597, 598)

Q.29 How was Christ's death 'redemptive'?

A. Christ was an innocent victim. He died, put to death as a criminal, although in no way did he deserve such a death. Throughout his whole life, there was no one who could ever 'convict him of sin'. No holier person ever existed. His cousin, John the Baptist, could point to him and say: 'Behold the Lamb of God, who takes away the sin of the world.'

The prophet Isaiah had foretold the death of the Messiah when he spoke of the Suffering Servant. In his death 'he bore the sins of many, and made intercession for the transgressors' (Isa 53:12).

In the Old Testament tradition, sins were 'taken away' by the offering of sacrifices to God, usually of animals or other food. The New Testament shows us Jesus using this same kind of language and accepting, willingly and freely, the role of the sacrificial lamb. In becoming 'true man' at the Incarnation he became subject to all the laws of physical, human life, including death. In St Matthew's Gospel, chapter 28, we find Jesus using the same language: 'The Son of man came . . . to give his life as a ransom.' (613f.)

The Second Person of the Holy Trinity, in assuming human nature, became one with us and, in solidarity with us, offered his life to the

Father in the sacrifice which surpasses all previous sacrifices. By his generous acceptance of death, our disobedience was replaced by his obedience; obedience to the Father who requires no more than that the freedom of human will, which is the root of all sin, is once more lovingly offered in obedience to its creator.

The Council of Trent says that Christ's sacrifice is 'the source of eternal salvation' which 'merited justification for us'. (617)

Q.30 What happened at the resurrection? Can the empty tomb be explained? Must Catholics believe in it?

A. It is certain that Jesus died on the cross. There were efforts, even from the very beginning, to claim that he had not died; that he had been taken down drugged and only presumed dead; that the crucifixion was a cleverly arranged illusion. None of these theories survived very long, even among his enemies. The fact that he died is rarely disputed now.

If the tomb was indeed empty, as his followers were convinced it was, that could have been explained in many ways: theft of the body (as some claimed at the time); Jesus' recovery from a coma; or an error as to where he had been laid. Nevertheless, the discovery of the empty tomb, although not in itself a proof of the resurrection, was certainly the first step in bringing the disciples to a realization that Jesus had risen from the dead as he had told them he would. Belief in the resurrection of Jesus is essential for Christians (otherwise, as St Paul said, our faith is meaningless). The gospels are unanimous in their account of the empty tomb, even if they vary in detail, as they do. If we doubt their witness, how can we say we believe Christ rose from the dead? On what could we base our faith?

What actually happened at the resurrection is certainly a great mystery. On the third day after the crucifixion, some of the disciples went to the burying-place to complete the anointing of Jesus' body, which could not be done earlier because of the Sabbath regulations. When they reached the tomb, the body was not there, although the grave-cloths in which it had been wrapped, were. (640, 643f.)

Nobody saw what happened at the resurrection. All we know is that those who had been closest to Jesus found that his body was no longer in the tomb where they knew he had been buried. Not only that, but within a very short time, those who had known him and been with him during his earthly life met him again, recognized him, spoke with him, and even ate with him (though some of them initially thought they were seeing a ghost). Whatever happened, a group of totally demoralized and frightened people – the followers of Jesus – were transformed into courageous witnesses to the risen Christ. As a result of their testimony, thousands of others were soon converted to their belief. The resurrection confirms that Jesus is alive and is God. (647, 653)

Through the testimony of his followers, all generations of Christians have believed that they too will, one day, rise from the dead. (624ff.)

Q.31 What is meant by the Second Coming?

A. After Jesus' death and resurrection, the gospels describe a period of forty days during which his disciples experienced his risen presence amongst them. At the end of this time he is described as returning to the Father when he was taken up into heaven at the Ascension. The Catechism describes what happened as 'the irreversible entry of his humanity into divine glory'. (659)

Since then we are in an interim stage which will last until the end of time. It is a period of waiting, during which Christ, through his Church, is to be preached to all nations, and a kingdom of justice and peace is to be established on earth. This is no easy task, as human history shows. But it is a task which must be undertaken untiringly. Meantime we are what the Second Vatican Council called 'a pilgrim people', on our way to that final day when Christ, in the words of the Creed, 'will come to judge the living and the dead'. St Luke, in his Gospel, says that Christ will come 'with great power and glory'. (673)

Nobody knows when this second coming of Christ will take place. Jesus told his disciples that only his Father knows; he will determine the right time. The book of Revelation describes the period of waiting as a time when the people will have to struggle with the powers of evil, which in turn will eventually be overcome by good on the Judgement Day, when God's greatness and goodness will be proclaimed in triumph. On that day, Jesus will confront each of us with our life, judging us by the law of love: 'As often as you did it to the least of my brethren, you did it to me.' (668ff., 675ff.)

Q.32 Who is the Holy Spirit?

A. The Holy Spirit is the Third Person of the Blessed Trinity. The Creed says that the Holy Spirit is adored and glorified together with the Father and the Son. As one of the Divine Persons, the Holy Spirit has existed from all eternity, but our knowledge has come gradually. The word 'spirit' itself is a translation of the Hebrew *ruach*, which means 'breath', 'air' or 'wind'. St John, in his Gospel, has Jesus describing the Spirit to Nicodemus in terms of wind.

The Spirit is often mentioned in the Old Testament, but never with the clarity that is found in the teachings of Jesus. The psalms ask God to send his Spirit on his people, and the prophecies of the Messiah often describe him as the one on whom the Spirit of the Lord will rest (Isaiah 11 and elsewhere). We know of the Spirit through the Scriptures (particularly in the teachings of Jesus and the apostles), through tradition, the Magisterium of the Church, the sacraments and through the holiness of the lives of the saints, both canonized and uncanonized. (702ff.)

It was through the power of the Spirit that Mary conceived. Jesus, her Son, promised to send the Spirit to guide the Church after he had returned to the Father. It is in the power of the same Holy Spirit that the Church continues its work and prayer to the end of time. The Catechism tells us that in order to have the Christian faith we must first have been touched by the Holy Spirit. (721)

The Holy Spirit is given a number of titles, each of which has a separate significance. Jesus often spoke of the Spirit, and the gospels instruct us to baptize in the name of the Father, Son and Holy Spirit. (693)

Jesus also uses the terms Paraclete and Advocate, Comforter and the Spirit of Truth to describe those aspects of the Spirit's work in the life of the believer. (692, 729)

The Church has many symbols to signify the Spirit, including water, oil, fire, wind, as on the first Pentecost, and, perhaps the most familiar of all, the dove. It was in this form that the Spirit was seen to descend on Jesus at his baptism and it is as a dove that Christian art most frequently shows the Spirit. (683ff., 694)

Q.33 What is the Catholic Church? Who belongs to it?

A. The word 'church' is a translation of the Greek word *ekklesia*, which is an assembly of people, called together for a particular purpose. In Christian tradition this 'calling together' is for the purpose of worship. Ever since sin entered the world, God has been calling people back to himself. Those who heard that call and responded to it in faith became the People of God, a title used throughout the Old Testament to mean the Jews. (751ff.)

Vatican II teaches that Christ, by preaching the good news of the Kingdom, inaugurated the Church, the new People of God. This community of faith is both a visible society of men and women and a spiritual community. The community is held together by the grace of the Holy Spirit, dwelling within it and guiding its members, under the headship of Jesus Christ its founder. This unity of the members with God is sustained by the Bread of Life, the Eucharist. The Church is also called the Body of Christ by St Paul, and the Mystical Body in Church documents. (781ff., 790ff.)

Traditionally, the Church is described as being one, holy, catholic and apostolic. It is *one*, in all its world-wide diversity, because it has one founder and is enlivened by the one Holy Spirit. It is *holy* because, although its members are imperfect and sinful, nevertheless they are sanctified by their sacramental contact with Christ. It is *catholic* (a word which means 'universal'), because, despite its diverse forms throughout the world, embracing, as it does, so many cultures, it is the same Christ who unites all its members. Its purpose is to preach the gospel of salvation and draw all people to Christ. (84ff., 813, 823, 830)

Finally, the Church is *apostolic*. This means that it was built on the foundation laid by Christ's apostles. Its message is that entrusted by him to the apostles, and it continues to be governed and guided by the bishops who are the successors of the apostles in the pastoral office. (857)

Who can belong to the Catholic Church? Anyone is a member of the Church who, under the grace of the Holy Spirit, accepts Jesus Christ as Lord, receives baptism in the name of the Father, Son and Holy Spirit, and who willingly accepts both the sacraments and the teaching of the Magisterium, and particularly the authority of the Pope. (748ff., 836)

Q.34 What is the Magisterium of the Church?

A. One of the most striking features of Jesus' teaching was that 'he taught with authority' and because of this, the crowds flocked to hear him. The pastors of the Church, namely the Pope and the bishops in communion with him, together with the theologians who help in their ministry, continue Christ's task of teaching. This task is more than a mere repetition of his teaching, however, since they must also proclaim the risen and glorified Christ, by whose inspiration and authority they continue to teach and guide the Church. By reason of their mission, they have the authority to do so. Magisterium is the name given to this authoritative teaching power, which is part of the essential foundation of the Church. (888ff.)

The Magisterium is exercised whenever the Church proclaims or explains moral or dogmatic truths, which can be traced through the centuries back to the time of the apostles, and when it makes laws and regulations based on the Law of God.

The pastors of the Church, being guided by the Holy Spirit, are protected from the danger of error in teaching the essentials of the faith. The Roman Pontiff, head of the College of Bishops, when *solemnly defining* moral or dogmatic truths to be held by all the faithful, can call on the Holy Spirit and in doing so is protected from error by the gift of infallibility, a gift that has not often been invoked. The Magisterium exists because of the *right* that all the faithful have to be guided in the truth. As with all rights, they have a corresponding duty to accept the teaching of the Magisterium. This does not mean, of course, that all theological discussion must cease. In matters of faith we are always faced with the problem of dealing with the Divine in merely human terms. Therefore there has to be a continual process whereby our understanding of the truths of faith is constantly deepened and renewed and expressed ever more clearly. (891, 892, 2030ff.)

Q.35 What is meant by the statement 'Outside the Church there is no salvation'?

A. This is a saying which has, through the years, been much misunderstood, and has made the Church seem arrogant. In a papal pronouncement (*Singulari Quidam*) of 1854, Pope Pius IX taught that it was an error to think that 'there is good hope for the eternal salvation of all those who do not in any way belong to the Church of Christ'. However, the Pope went on in the same document to say that he in no way meant to 'set limits to the divine mercy, which is infinite'. (846)

With the passing of the years, the apparent harshness of such teaching has been softened in many official Church documents, most notably in the teaching of Vatican II, where the positive values of other religions are recognized and even celebrated.

The Catechism prefers to interpret the doctrine in a positive way; all salvation comes through Christ. He is the head of the Church, his Mystical Body. So, insofar as the Church is the embodiment of Christ, all salvation comes through the Church.

This does not mean that those who are not members of the Church cannot be saved. Jesus did say that salvation would come through faith and baptism. But this can only apply to those who have had the opportunity to come to the truth, who could have believed and been baptized and who have not deliberately rejected Christ and his Church. On the other hand, to condemn those who, through no fault of their own, may never have come to a realization of that truth, or who may have been genuinely mistaken as to the truth, would clearly be unjust. God cannot act unjustly, nor should his Church. Therefore the Church teaches that all people of good will, who seek God with a sincere heart, in accordance with their conscience, can be saved.

It follows that it is the task of the Church, under the guidance of the Holy Spirit, to work untiringly to bring the gospel to the ends of the earth. The Church is necessarily, therefore, a missionary Church. Many errors have been committed in the past in the pursuit of this missionary vision. There have been most regrettable instances of forced conversions, etc. However, today the Church sees itself as engaged in what the Catechism calls 'respectful dialogue' with other Christian churches and with those who do not yet accept the gospel. (846ff., 856)

Q.36 What is the Communion of Saints?

A. The Communion of Saints is, in a word, the Church. It is not just the Church of today, but of all who have ever been members. All those who have ever been linked sacramentally with Christ, the head, are therefore linked to one another as members of his body. The Communion of Saints then, is a communion of sharing with members united in a shared faith, shared sacraments, shared gifts of the Holy Spirit and a shared concern and responsibility for one another, in both their physical and spiritual needs. (946ff.)

Those sharing this communion include the saints in heaven, led by Mary, the mother of Jesus, who never cease interceding for those on earth, and also those who, although not yet in glory, have died and are awaiting the beatific vision. The Church teaches that they too can pray for us, just as we can pray for them.

The word 'saints' is even applied to those of us still struggling on earth. St Paul, in his letters, often refers to the Church members as saints. This means that we, because we belong to the Church, are bound to strive to be holy and worthy of Christ, Our Lord. (897, 946f.)

Q.37 What is the life of the world to come? Will we survive as individuals?

A. The life of the world to come is our true destiny. Life here on earth is but a preparation for it. The Second Council of Lyons (1274) taught that the Roman Church firmly believes and confesses that on the Day of Judgement everyone will appear in their own bodies before Christ in all his glory to give an account of their own life. Jesus, in St Matthew's Gospel (25:31–46), describes the scene: 'He will place the sheep at his right hand but the goats at the left. Then the king will say to those at his right hand, "Come, blessed of my Father, inherit the kingdom prepared for you from the foundation of the world; for I was hungry and you gave me food; I was thirsty and you gave me drink; I was a stranger and you welcomed me; I was naked and you clothed me; I was sick and you visited me; I was in prison and you came to me. . . . as you did it to one of the least of these my brethren, you did it to me" . . . Those who did not do any of these things will go away into eternal punishment, but the righteous into eternal life.'

It has been the constant teaching of the Church, based on the words of Christ himself and the Scriptures, that after death, our spirits will survive, being immortal, and that, at the last day, they will be reunited with our bodies. He said 'I am the resurrection and the life' (John 11:25). (997)

How exactly our resurrection will take place, no one knows. All we do know is that God who created us will, one day, reunite our bodies with our souls. (992ff., 997)

If we believe that Christ is risen from the dead and is with his Father, body and soul, then it is our belief and our hope that an eternal destiny like his awaits us too. After his resurrection, the apostles not only saw him, but ate and drank with him and, at his urging, touched him to prove that he was no mere ghost or phantom, but real flesh and bone.

Belief in the resurrection of the dead has been an essential element of Christian faith from the beginning. St Paul in his first letter to the Corinthians (15:12–14, 20) says 'How can some of you say there is no resurrection of the dead? But if there is no resurrection of the dead, then Christ has not been raised; if Christ has not been raised, then our preaching is in vain and your faith is in vain ... But in fact Christ has been raised from the dead, the first fruits of those who have fallen asleep.'

St John, in his Gospel, says 'Eternal life is this: to know you, the only true God, and Jesus Christ whom you have sent' (John 17:3).

Our resurrection will, itself, be part of that great phenomenon, the new creation which is foretold in the Bible. At the end of time, all creation will be renewed. Scripture says there will be 'new heavens and a new earth'. Until that day of renewal our comprehension of what will happen is necessarily incomplete. Nevertheless, as we say in the Creed, that does not deter us from firmly believing and hoping 'in the life of the world to come'. (1042ff.)

Q.38 Why do Catholics pray for the souls of the dead?

A. In the case of those who die in the state of grace, who have not excluded God and his love from their lives, but who are as yet not fully freed from their sins, however venial, the Church teaches that they will pass through a state of purification, which is traditionally called purgatory. In this state they can be helped and their 'time' (to use human terms) in purgatory can be shortened by the intercessions and prayers of those of us still on earth. This is the basis of the practice of praying for the dead, that they may be released from the punishment due to sin. (1030ff.)

The practice of praying for the dead existed long before Christianity. The second book of Maccabees, in the Old Testament, tells how Judas Maccabeus, leader of the Israelite army and a holy man, after a battle, prayed and made offerings for the dead soldiers 'that they might be delivered from their sin' (2 Macc 2:46). (1032) Ch. 2 v, 43 - 45

From the beginning, the Church has honoured the dead and prayed for them, particularly in the sacrifice of the Mass, offered on their behalf. Other good works, such as almsgiving and acts of penance, are also considered beneficial to the souls in purgatory.

The practice of interceding for the souls of the departed reaches its highest form in the celebration of the Requiem Mass on the occasion of funerals and anniversaries. Some of the world's greatest composers have made musical settings of the Requiem, which are regarded not just as works of art but also as supreme acts of faith in the power of prayer to help the souls of the departed.

On the feast of All Souls, 2 November, every year the Catholic Church celebrates and honours in a special way all those who have died, by offering Requiem Masses and other prayers for the repose of their souls. The most frequently used prayer for the dead asks: 'Eternal rest grant unto them, O Lord, let perpetual light shine upon them. May their souls and the souls of all the faithful departed, through the mercy of God, rest in peace. Amen.' The inscription 'RIP' often found on the tombstones of Christians means *Requiescant in pace*, Latin for 'may they rest in peace'. (1030ff.)

Q.39 What are heaven and hell?

A. It is best to start with heaven since God made all human beings to be with him there. Heaven, a word used many times in the Scriptures and by Christ, is best described as a state or way of existing in the presence of God. Pope Benedict XII, in the year 1336, defined that 'the souls of all the saints and other faithful who die in God's grace have been, are and will be in heaven, in the heavenly kingdom and the celestial paradise with Christ . . .'.

St Paul, in his first letter to the Corinthians, said that 'eye has not seen, nor ear heard, nor has the heart of man conceived what God has prepared for those who love him' (1 Cor 2:9). The Catechism describes heaven as 'This mystery of blessed communion with God and all who are in Christ'. When we reach heaven, God will reveal himself to us in all his glory. This is what is called the beatific vision, the experience of total happiness. It is for this, after all, that God created us in the first place. Our life here on earth is but a pilgrimage, a journey characterized by hope. (1023)

What, then, of hell? Hell is a state of being eternally separated from God and from all who are united with him in love. The Scriptures and Jesus himself often spoke of hell, usually in terms of fire, although it is thought that the greatest pain of hell would be the experience of eternal separation from God. All Jesus' teaching, in one way or another, is concerned with living so that eventually we may be united with him, the Father and the Spirit, and thus avoid the possibility of eternal separation from them. It is not God's will that anyone should end up in hell. The Church has never taught that any particular individual has gone to hell, preferring, rather, to trust and hope in the divine love and mercy. But since we are free creatures, it is possible, in theory at least, that someone could obstinately persist in a state of deliberate mortal sin, fully realizing what this meant. Such positive rejection or hatred of God and his redeeming love would exclude the sinner from eternal happiness. It is because of this awesome possibility that the Church, in the liturgy, constantly asks that we may 'be saved from final damnation and be counted among the chosen'. (1033ff., 1037)

PART TWO

THE CELEBRATION OF THE CHRISTIAN MYSTERY

Q.40 What does the word 'liturgy' mean?

A. The word 'liturgy' comes from the Greek *leiton ergon*, which means 'public work', or 'public service'. The Christian churches speak of liturgy as the public response to our knowledge of God. It is expressed in worship and in other activities, such as the proclamation of the gospel and living the gospel ideals in our daily lives. (1069)

The need for liturgy is rooted in the social nature of human beings. It is not sufficient for each of us to act alone; we are related in our common humanity, and therefore certain activities need to be shared with others.

Vatican II speaks of liturgy as the central act in the life of the Church. In the liturgy, especially in the Mass, 'the work of our redemption is accomplished'. In a mysterious way, the liturgy combines both the human and the divine: God and people coming together in a shared action. The Church teaches that, through their baptism, the faithful share in the priesthood of Christ. Their offerings and prayers are joined to his most perfect offering of himself to the Father.

All liturgical activity is connected to the proclamation of the gospel. For this reason the Church has traditionally said *Lex orandi, lex credendi*, or, broadly translated, our prayer is based on our belief, and our belief conditions the way we pray.

From the very beginning, the Church has carried out a 'liturgical catechesis'; that is to say, by taking part in the liturgy, people are being instructed in the faith, through Bible readings and sermons and by being reminded of the great central mysteries of redemption as they are celebrated in prayer and music. Through their celebration of Christ in the Eucharist and the other sacraments, their faith, both individually and as a community, is deepened and renewed. (1074)

The Catechism urges us to study the worship of the Jews as a step to a fuller understanding of Catholic liturgy. Both religions hold sacred Scripture as essential to their prayer and every aspect of Christian liturgy has a parallel in Jewish worship. (1066–1075, 1093)

Q.41 Why do we speak of 'celebrating' the Mass and the sacraments?

A. To celebrate is to rejoice in, or mark, a special event with festivities. It is a joyful notion. The Catechism quotes from the Apocalypse of St John, the book of Revelation. There the writer describes his vision of the blessed spirits in heaven, the heavenly powers (angels), all created nature, God's special servants in both Old and New Testaments, those who have come to the new Christian faith and have died as martyrs, the Mother of God and, finally, 'a great multitude which no one could number, from every nation, from all tribes and peoples and tongues'. This great multitude is described as being engaged in the joyous worship or celebration of the Father and the Lamb, Jesus who was slain and has risen.

Because of the presence among them of the Holy Spirit, the Church sees its members on earth as sharing, in a limited way, in this heavenly celebration. Through the centuries of Christian tradition there has developed an impressive body of art, music and sacred texts, all produced by and portraying the faithful sharing in the eternal worship. (1156)

As the Catechism says, the meaning of liturgical signs and symbols is rooted in the work of creation and in human culture ... God speaks to us through the visible creation. Light and darkness, wind and fire, water and earth, trees and their fruits, all speak to us of their creator. (1145ff.)

The faithful, in their turn, can take these things and dedicate them to the worship of God, as they can with other human activities; washing and anointing, sharing food – all can express the sanctifying presence of and our gratitude towards our creator. In this way, human words, music and artifacts are woven into a rich tapestry of celebration.

Quoting St John Damascene, the Catechism says 'The beauty of the images moves me to contemplation, as a meadow delights the eyes and subtly infuses the soul with the glory of God'. So, too, the contemplation of sacred images, music and texts in the context of worship leads to an experience that should lift the soul to a true celebration. (1136ff., 1159ff.)

Q.42 What do we mean by the liturgical year?

A. From the earliest times, it has been the custom of human beings to commemorate the significant events in their history. Under Moses, the Israelites celebrated the *mirabilia Dei*, the wonders of God, those things in which the people saw the hand of God guiding their destiny. So, for example, the people annually celebrated Passover, their delivery from slavery in Egypt, when the angel of death had 'passed over' their homes. (1163f.)

The supreme celebration for Christians is that of the resurrection of Christ, which is recalled every Sunday of the year, but especially at Easter, which Vatican II calls the 'most solemn of all feasts'. The rest of the festivals throughout the remainder of the liturgical year unfold various aspects of the Easter mystery. (1168ff.)

Throughout the year various feasts are celebrated: feasts of the Lord, the Blessed Virgin and the other saints.

Every day of the year is blessed by having its own liturgy, made up of:

- The *Liturgy of the Hours*, where, seven times in the day, the Lord is honoured by readings from Scripture, the recitation of psalms, the singing of hymns and prayers of intercession. The Liturgy of the Hours has been traditionally the vocation of the monastic orders, whose members, in their monasteries and convents, prayed for the welfare of the rest of the Church outside their cloisters. Today, particularly since Vatican II, these prayers are more and more frequently being celebrated in parish churches too. (1174)
- The *Eucharist*, as the crown and summit of all the Church's liturgy, is often celebrated on weekdays as well as on Sundays, though, of course, on weekdays there is no obligation on the faithful to attend. Nevertheless, many people are happy to attend Mass on a daily basis. (1322ff.)

By whom is the liturgy celebrated? By the whole Church, acting as one community. 'Wherever two or three are gathered in my name . . .' as Jesus said. Normally there is someone to preside at the celebration, and in most cases it is a member of the clergy, whose particular vocation this is. But even in the absence of clergy, lay people can lead the Christian community in prayer and give and receive

Holy Communion using previously consecrated hosts. (1140ff.)

Where should the liturgy be celebrated? God can be praised wherever believers are gathered together. But where possible, Christians have built special places consecrated to worship. These churches serve not just as shelter to the praying community, but as signs of the presence of God among his people. (1179ff.)

Q.43 The Catechism constantly uses the word 'paschal'. What does this mean?

A. The word 'paschal' is an adjective derived from the Hebrew noun 'Pasch'. It refers to the Jewish feast of Passover, which celebrates the escape of the people of Israel from slavery in Egypt, described in the book of Exodus. It was this central festival that Christ and his disciples were celebrating in Jerusalem when the tragic events of what we know as Holy Week unfolded. They had gone up to Jerusalem 'to celebrate the Pasch'. Every year, to the present day, the Jewish people celebrate that event with a meal which includes unleavened bread, and wine. The ceremonies of the Mass, also centred on bread and wine, are similarly called 'paschal'. The whole drama of Jesus' death and resurrection is 'the paschal mystery'. Through his death and resurrection Christ brought a new deliverance from death and the power of sin. Because of this, his triumph is sometimes called a 'New Passover'. The shared use of the word 'Pasch' in both Jewish and Christian theology and worship indicates how closely the two religions are related in their background and roots. (1085ff.)

It is important to know that the word 'mystery' in the context of the faith does not have the connotations that it has acquired in recent times; it does not mean something magic or occult. Rather, it retains its earlier meaning of something holy or to be revered. So, the priest, at the beginning of Mass, invites the congregation to celebrate the 'sacred mysteries'. In this sense, the word 'mystery' occurs often in the liturgy and the Catechism.

It was in the sacrificial death of Christ, and his resurrection, that the history of salvation reached its peak. The fruits of Jesus' redemptive work continue to be effective in the lives of the faithful through the celebration of the sacraments, especially the sacrament of the Eucharist.

In this, all three persons of the Holy Trinity are active. The *Father* is the author and source of all that is. He fills his creation with countless blessings, sanctifying everything, especially those who have found faith in his sacraments. Jesus, the Incarnate *Son* of the Father, communicates his many graces and blessings on the faithful through his gospel and sacraments. The *Holy Spirit* 'prepares the Church to encounter her Lord' and with transforming power makes the mystery of Christ present, with his Church here and now. (1076ff., 1084ff., 1093)

Q.44 What is a sacrament? How many sacraments are there? How is Christ present in the sacraments?

A. A sacrament is an action of the Holy Spirit at work in the Church. It is also a type of symbol, a sign which brings to mind something other than itself. For example, a red traffic light symbolizes, or brings to mind, the danger involved in not stopping. For a symbol to be a sacrament, however, it must not simply bring something to mind, but it must actually cause the thing symbolized to come into being. Therefore, sacraments are signs *which cause that which they symbolize to come into being.* And that which they symbolize is God's grace. Every sacrament causes an increase of grace in those who receive it worthily. (1116, 1127)

The prime example of a sacrament, in Catholic theology, is the Eucharist. In the Eucharist, the consecration of the bread and wine does not simply symbolize the Last Supper of Christ with his disciples, but actually brings about the living presence of Christ in the bread and wine and in those who celebrate the Eucharist.

As will be clear later, each sacrament confers its own special grace. Nevertheless, all sacraments share one thing: they make Christ present with those who celebrate them in faith.

Today, in the light of centuries of prayer and study, the Church teaches that there are seven sacraments. Each one symbolizes in a special way the presence of Christ with his faithful at crucial stages in their Christian lives, building and strengthening them as a community.

The seven sacraments of the Catholic Church are:

Sacraments of initiation

1 *Baptism*: celebrated as the first step in the initiation of a believer into the community of faith.
2 *Confirmation*: the second sacrament of Christian initiation bringing the believer into adult Christian life.
3 *Eucharist*: the crown and summit of all the sacraments, in which Christ gives himself, under the symbolic signs of bread and wine, as the 'daily bread' of the faithful, strengthening them in their everyday lives.

Sacraments of healing

4 *Penance*, or the *sacrament of reconciliation*, in which the Christian, acknowledging his or her sins, and being sorry for them, is forgiven and is received back into full communion with Christ. (1480ff.)
5 *Anointing*: primarily for healing and strengthening, in which the sick and dying are given the grace to endure their suffering and, where appropriate, given the strength with which to face death and the journey to eternal life with all their sins forgiven. (1511)

Sacraments of communion

6 *Holy orders*: in this sacrament, chosen people are consecrated for the preaching of the gospel, the administration of the sacraments and, above all, to preside at the celebration of the Eucharist. (1536ff.)
7 *Matrimony*: the sacrament by which a man and a woman consecrate themselves to one another and to the Christian community to ensure membership of the Church from generation to generation. (1601ff.)

Baptism, confirmation and holy orders are said to have a special and permanent effect on those who receive them. This is sometimes expressed as imprinting a special character on the soul. Because of this permanence, these sacraments are never repeated.

Q.45 What is the role of the Holy Spirit in the sacraments?

A. Since the first Pentecost, with its dramatic outpouring of the Holy Spirit on the apostles in the form of fire and the gift of tongues, the

Holy Spirit has been understood as the primary communication of the Godhead in its dealings with humanity. This is never more true than when it comes to the celebration of the sacraments.

As the Spirit of Truth and the Spirit of Wisdom, the Holy Spirit is the one who prepares, through God's grace, the minds and hearts of the faithful gathered to worship, and helps them understand those Old Testament texts and events that can be seen, with Christian hindsight, to have both foreshadowed and been fulfilled in the Christian mysteries. The Spirit has been called 'the Church's living memory'. (1099)

The first covenant between God and his people, the Exodus, the Passover, the exile and return are all seen to have their counterpart in the Christian mysteries. The flood, with Noah and his Ark, the crossing of the Red (or Reed) Sea, the water flowing from the rock at Meribah and the manna in the desert are all prophecies-in-action, of the Christian sacraments.

Through the inspired words of the Scripture readings, the psalms and the prayers of the liturgy, the Holy Spirit speaks to the hearts of the worshipping community. Through the Spirit's grace, they are led to make that 'response of faith' to what they hear, so that in turn they may, with ever increasing devotion, benefit from the sacraments which they receive. (1100)

Of all the sacraments, confirmation is seen as one which particularly celebrates the Holy Spirit, whose seven gifts are given in this sacrament. They are wisdom, understanding, counsel, fortitude, piety, knowledge and fear of the Lord.

There is also a special moment in the celebration of the Eucharist when the priest, holding his hands extended over the bread and wine, invites the Holy Spirit to come upon the gifts and change them into Christ's body and blood. (1105-1109)

The Catechism quotes St John Damascene: 'You ask how the bread becomes the Body of Christ, and the wine ... the Blood of Christ. I shall tell you: the Holy Spirit comes upon them and accomplishes what surpasses every word and thought ... Let it be enough for you to understand that it is by the Holy Spirit, just as it was of the Holy Virgin and by the Holy Spirit that the Lord, through and in himself, took flesh.' (1106)

Q.46 What is baptism?

A. Baptism is the sacrament which is the basis of the whole Christian life, the gateway to life in the Holy Spirit and the door which allows us to celebrate the other sacraments. (1213)

As a sacrament it is a sacred and symbolic act which makes a person a member of the Church of Christ and to share in the graces and blessings which the Church offers to all its members. It is also the first of the sacraments known as the sacraments of initiation, which bring people into the life of the Church. The other sacraments of initiation are confirmation and Eucharist.

The word 'baptism' comes from the Greek *baptizein,* which means to plunge or immerse (in water). All sacraments take some common element (bread, wine, oil, water ...) and enrich it with a special significance which makes it sacramental and enables it to give the grace which it symbolizes. (1214)

Baptism, which brings salvation through the use of water, was foreshadowed in the Old Testament accounts of Noah's Ark and the crossing of the Red Sea. In each case, faithful people were saved from destruction by passing through or across water. (1217ff.)

In the New Testament, John the Baptist's rite of washing in the Jordan, which Jesus himself chose to undergo in order to signify his oneness with his people, is also seen as prefiguring the Christian sacrament. (1224)

Baptism purifies those who receive it from all sin, whether actually committed (if they are adult and therefore capable of personal sin) or inherited (i.e. original sin) if they are babies. Further, baptism fills the soul with grace, making it a 'dwelling place of the Holy Spirit' and uniting the person with the risen Christ. Finally, it unites the baptized with all other members of Christ's Church, with whom they share both the divine life of grace and the hope of eternal life.

An age-old custom encourages the naming of the new Christian on the occasion of baptism. This is known as christening. The new Christian is given and accepts a name associated with some Christian virtue (Faith, or Constance, for instance) or one of the saints. From that day, they are considered to be, in a special way, under the protection of that saint, who is called their patron saint.

Can anyone receive this sacrament? Yes, provided they are prepared, normally through instruction, to accept Christ as their Lord and are willing to subscribe to the Christian Creed. In the case of infants, they are baptized because of the shared faith of the community presenting them for baptism. There must be an assurance that, in due course, they will be educated in the faith of the Church. This responsibility is shared between parents, godparents and teachers. (1246ff.)

In the Gospel of Matthew (28:19) Jesus states that baptism is necessary for salvation and instructs his disciples to go out and proclaim the gospel to all nations and to baptize them. What then of those who have never heard the gospel preached? Are they damned? No, this would clearly be unjust. The Church teaches that it is God's will that everyone be saved. Therefore, if someone never had the opportunity to hear the gospel or know of Christ, they will not be condemned for something that was not their fault. Traditionally, the Church speaks of *baptism of desire* for those who wished for baptism but who died before they could receive it, and *baptism of blood*, which refers to those non-Christians, perhaps those preparing for baptism, who lost their lives in persecutions throughout history. (1257)

Q.47 What is confirmation?

A. Confirmation is a sacrament whereby a Christian is given an increase of baptismal grace and is strengthened by the Holy Spirit to live an adult Christian life, accepting and proclaiming the truths of the Catholic Church.

The sacrament is given through anointing with oil and the laying-on of hands, normally by a bishop. The holy oil is called chrism and is consecrated once a year, on Holy Thursday, at a special cathedral ceremony. The word 'chrism' itself echoes the name Christ, which is simply a word that means 'the anointed one'. The use of chrism in sacraments throughout a diocese during the rest of the year is a powerful sign of the link that all parishes have with their bishop and cathedral. (1297ff.)

On many occasions, Jesus promised the gift of the Holy Spirit to his disciples. On the first Pentecost his promise was fulfilled. Inspired and emboldened by the Holy Spirit they went out full of courage to proclaim the gospel. Such was their courage and enthusiasm that, Scripture tells us, they converted three thousand souls to Christ on one day.

Pope Paul VI, quoted in the Catechism, says: '... the apostles, in fulfilment of Christ's will, imparted to the newly baptized, by the laying on of hands, the gift of the Spirit that completes the grace of Baptism. For this reason, in the *Letter to the Hebrews* the doctrine concerning Baptism and the laying on of hands is listed among the first elements of Christian instruction. The imposition of hands is recognized by the Catholic tradition as the origin of the sacrament of Confirmation, which in a certain way perpetuates the grace of Pentecost in the Church.' (1288)

In the early years of the Church, baptism and confirmation were normally given on the same occasion. St Cyprian called such celebrations a 'double sacrament'. This practice still continues in the Eastern Churches. In the Western Church, the two sacraments have become separated, baptism being given by a priest or even, in emergency, by anybody else, whilst confirmation was postponed until a time when it was convenient for the bishop to be present for the ceremony. In the Western Church, both sacraments are often celebrated on the same occasion in the case of adults joining the Church.

Normally, confirmation is given by the bishop, signifying the union between the sacrament, the person receiving it, and the Church of the apostles, whose successors the bishops are. In the case of emergency, however, confirmation may be administered by a priest representing the bishop. (1285ff., 1290)

Q.48 What is the Eucharist?

A. The Eucharist is the third of the sacraments of Christian initiation. It is also the chief of all the sacraments. The Catechism calls it 'the summary of all our faith' and 'the centre of the Church's life'. Those who have been baptized and confirmed participate, through this sacrament, in the sacrifice of the Lord. (1324ff.)

Jesus instituted the Eucharist when he and his disciples celebrated the start of the important Jewish feast of Passover. This was also the night on which he was to be betrayed by Judas Iscariot. During the meal, he broke some bread, said a blessing over it and gave it to his disciples. As he did so, he spoke words which must have amazed his hearers. He said, of the bread, 'Take this and eat. This is my body ...' And again, taking the cup of wine, he said 'Take and drink. This is the cup of my blood which is given for you.' Then he told them to 'do this in memory of me'. (1334)

In Jewish religious practice, to do something 'in memory' has a special meaning. It does not simply mean to remember, but rather, to 'make present'. To this day, when Jewish families celebrate Passover they understand that, in some mysterious way, the events of the original Exodus, when their forebears, led by Moses, passed through the sea and escaped from slavery in Egypt, are once again made present. (1337)

Catholics believe that, during the celebration of the Eucharist, the bread and wine, consecrated and offered to God by the priest, become, in a mysterious way beyond human understanding, the body and blood of Christ, while retaining the visible forms of bread and wine.

The Council of Trent said that in the bread and wine of the Eucharist, 'the body and blood, soul and divinity of Our Lord Jesus Christ, and therefore the whole Christ, is truly, really and substantially contained'. This is known as 'trans-substantiation'. (1374, 1376)

The Eucharist makes present the one sacrifice of Christ on the cross. On Calvary he gave himself willingly for others. In the Eucharist he continues to give himself as the very words show. 'This is my body which *is given* for you ... This cup which *is poured out* for you ...' (1362ff.)

This is why we speak of the *Real Presence* of Christ in the Eucharistic bread and wine. This presence begins at the moment of the consecration of the bread and wine and remains as long as the sacred host and wine continue to subsist. This explains why Catholics revere the reserved sacrament, the consecrated host which is kept in the tabernacle in churches and oratories, as the real living presence of Christ.

Those who worthily receive the Eucharist are united with Christ and with one another and are given a renewed pledge of eternal life.

It is important, if we are to accept the Lord's invitation, that we are properly prepared to receive him. Out of respect for the Bread of Life, a period of one hour's fast from food and drink should normally be observed before receiving communion. This does not apply to the elderly or those who are ill. (1377ff.)

It is also necessary that any serious sins which have not yet been forgiven in the sacrament of reconciliation should be confessed. (1415)

Holy Communion given at the time of death is called viaticum (Latin for '[that which is for you] on the way'). (1524f.)

Q.49 How is the Eucharist celebrated?

A. From as early as the second century we have a description, by St Justin Martyr, of the way the Eucharist should be celebrated. The outline of the ceremony has changed remarkably little in the course of the years. What takes place in any church or cathedral on a Sunday morning at the end of the twentieth century could, without much difficulty, be recognized by a Christian from the early Church. (1345)

The Christian assembly comes together at a given hour to gather around the 'two tables' of the word and the sacrament. The celebration begins with the Liturgy of the Word. Selected passages from the Old and New Testaments are read aloud and are explained in a homily or sermon which is followed by a 'bidding prayer' in which the intentions of the community are read out and prayed for. Then the community proclaim their faith in the words of one of the great creeds, the Nicene or the Apostles'. (1348f.)

The Liturgy of the Word is followed by the offertory, when the bread and wine for the Eucharist are presented at the altar, together with the collection. These funds provide a living for the clergy and are also used for charitable donations and for the upkeep of the church. (1350f.)

The Liturgy of the Sacrament follows. It is centred on one of several *Eucharistic Prayers*, all similar in structure, being based on the gospel accounts of the Last Supper. At the centre of the prayer are the Lord's own words: the consecration or words of 'institution'. They are surrounded with prayers to the Holy Spirit, intercessions for both the living and the dead, and, in conclusion, all join in the Lord's Prayer before receiving Holy Communion. (1352ff.)

At Communion, the consecrated bread and wine are received by both clergy and congregation, who recognize in the eating and drinking that they are reunited in a special way with the risen and living Lord, truly present in the bread and wine. (1355)

Finally, the priest blesses the congregation and sends them out to proclaim the gospel in their daily lives. The Latin word *Missa* means 'sent' and from this we get the word 'Mass', which is frequently used by Catholics for the Eucharist. (1332)

Q.50 What is the sacrament of reconciliation or confession? Why is it needed? Who can forgive sins? Can every sin be forgiven?

A. St John in his Gospel reminds us that we are all sinners and that we fool ourselves if we deny this. Therefore we continually need God's forgiveness which comes to us in this sacrament.

Sin damages our relationship with God and with the Church community. In the normal course of events, both the sinner and the wider community are entitled to some public and recognizable *sign* that sins have been forgiven and that people are reconciled to God and to one another. It is this public sign of forgiveness and reconciliation that we call the sacrament of penance, reconciliation or confession.

In confession, the sinner confesses his or her sins before a minister of the church (bishop or priest) with sorrow and determination, as far as possible, not to sin again. They are then absolved from sin, restored to the grace of God (where that grace may have been lost by grave sin), welcomed back to full communion with the Church and undertake to make amends for any damage or injury done. Some act of penance is given by the priest, such as prayer, almsgiving or some other good act, which helps to restore spiritual health. This sacrament can bring a great feeling of peace and relief with the removal of guilt. (1448)

Jesus Christ, during his earthly ministry, not only forgave sinners, but also instructed his disciples to do so, when he told them 'Whose sins you shall forgive, they are forgiven. Whose sins you shall retain, they are retained' (John 20:23). In the prayer which he left us, the Lord's Prayer, he tells us to ask God to forgive us our sins, as we forgive those who sin against us. It follows that if we cannot forgive those who injure us, it is presumptuous for us to ask forgiveness from God. (1443ff.)

But why, if God is love, and if the sinners can turn to him in sorrow, in the secrecy of their hearts, is this sacrament necessary? There is no doubt that the forgiving love of God exists, and existed, from all eternity and therefore before any sacrament was ever thought of. Certainly, too, if, for whatever reason, the truly contrite sinner has no access to the sacrament, but turns to God for forgiveness, it is inconceivable that the God of infinite mercy and love would not grant it. (1434ff.)

It is God alone who forgives sins and restores the life of grace to the soul of the sinner, and in the sacrament of reconciliation this is done through the ministry of the priest in the name of the Blessed Trinity.

The words of absolution, spoken by the priest, are:

God, the Father of mercies,
through the death and resurrection of his Son,
has reconciled the world to himself
and sent the Holy Spirit among us
for the forgiveness of sins;
through the ministry of the Church
may God give you pardon and peace,
and I absolve you from your sins
in the name of the Father, and of the Son, and of the Holy Spirit.
    (1449)

There is no sin that cannot be forgiven *provided that there is true sorrow*. Where Jesus in the gospel speaks of 'the sin against the Holy Ghost' it is taken to mean that even God is 'powerless' to forgive the sinners who persist in turning their backs on the grace of the Holy Spirit and refuse to be sorry for things which they truly realize are wrong. The Church, as representing Christ, claims, however, to be able to forgive all sinners even if they should continue sinning until the last day of their lives, provided that they can at last summon up an act of contrition, however imperfect. (1864)

Before we receive Holy Communion, the Church urges us to receive this sacrament if we are conscious of any unforgiven grave sin. (1423)

Q.51 What are indulgences? Do they still exist? Were they not one of the causes of the Reformation?

A. To deal with the second question first, it was not the doctrine of indulgences that was the problem, but rather the *apparent selling* of them. The faithful were, in some cases, being asked to make financial offerings for various good causes, including the building of the basilica of St Peter's in Rome. In return they were being assured of a pardon for souls in purgatory. Inevitably this led to misunderstanding on the part of some, and even to exploitation of the more simple by the unscrupulous. But whatever pious explanations may have been offered, the fact is that money was being asked in return for something that money cannot buy. The attempt to buy or sell spiritual things is known as simony, after the magician Simon who, as told in the Acts of the Apostles, tried to buy spiritual power from St Peter and was cursed for it.

This brings us back to indulgences themselves. To understand them it is necessary to understand that sin has a *double consequence*: one is the loss of grace (which, unrestored, could lead to eternal punishment), the other is what the Catechism calls 'an unhealthy attachment to creatures, which must be purified either here on earth, or after death in the state called Purgatory'. (1472)

When sin is forgiven, for instance in the sacrament of reconciliation, grace is restored and eternal punishment is remitted, but temporal punishment remains. This in turn is remitted by prayer, works of mercy and charity. Nowadays, indulgences do not involve money but they can still be granted upon the saying of certain prayers or doing certain good works.

Because of that union between all the faithful which we call the Communion of Saints, people are able to pray for others whether they are living or dead. Thus, the prayers, works of mercy etc. of one person can benefit another. This is the idea underlying the doctrine of indulgences. (1474)

Q.52 Why are the sick anointed?

A. During his life on earth, Jesus cured many sick people. He did this both as an act of love and mercy and to show that physical, spiritual and psychological ills can be cured by God's grace. His disciples, too, are described as preaching repentance, and anointing the sick with oil and healing them (cf. Mark 6:12–13). In his epistle, St James instructs the presbyters (i.e. priests) of the Church to anoint the sick so that they may be cured and their sins forgiven (cf. James 5:14–15). (1503ff.)

The sacrament of anointing, therefore, is intended for those who are ill, very frail or dying. Over the centuries, anointing tended to be reserved for those who were terminally ill, which gave rise to the name 'extreme unction'.

Today, while the sacrament is still given to those who are close to death (in which case its function is to strengthen and calm the dying person, as well as forgiving their sins), the healing and calming power of the sacrament is available to all who are seriously ill, whether at the point of death or not. It may be repeated for every new illness or, indeed, any significant worsening of the original illness. (1514f.)

Anointing is given in the context of a Liturgy of the Word: a suitable passage of Scripture is read, the minister gently lays hands upon the patient, whilst praying to the Holy Spirit. Then the patient is anointed with holy oil. Normally this has been blessed by the bishop during the ceremonies of Holy Week and so it symbolizes the union between this patient and the Christian community. It also provides a fitting end to the other anointings of Christian life which began with baptism. (1517ff.)

As a result of this sacrament, the Holy Spirit strengthens and consoles the sick, the patient is more closely united with Christ and his redemptive sufferings, with the rest of the faithful in the Body of Christ, the Church, and, if terminally ill, is strengthened for the final journey to the 'heavenly homeland'. In a delightful pastoral insight, the old Roman Catechism (the Catechism of the Council of Trent) describes this sacrament as helping the sick person 'cheerfully to await the Lord's coming'.

The sacrament of anointing is often given together with viaticum (the Eucharist) at the time of death. However, even when there is no immediate danger of death, the sick should be encouraged to call the priest and receive this sacrament. (1499ff.)

Q.53 What is the sacrament of holy orders? Who can receive it? How do clergy differ from the laity?

A. Jesus appointed his apostles to continue his redemptive ministry to the end of time. Those who receive this sacrament are, therefore, linked by a special grace to Christ, the apostles and their successors, the bishops, in proclaiming the teaching of Jesus and trying to bring God's Kingdom on earth. (1537)

In ancient times, the Latin word *ordo* indicated a group of people who were to serve or govern the community. In the Church, *ordo* or order was applied to individuals who gave themselves to serve the whole church community for their instruction and sanctification. From the earliest times, the orders were divided into three: bishops, priests and deacons.

The notion of priesthood itself comes from the Old Testament. God chose the members of the tribe of Levi to be his special ministers to lead the people in worship, proclaim his Word and offer sacrifices in the

Temple. The Church sees, in the service of the sons of Levi, a foreshadowing of the priesthood of the New Testament. (1541)

Jesus is the one eternal and perfect priest; the one mediator between God and humanity. In the mystery of the incarnation, being both God and man, Jesus is the perfect meeting-point of Godhead and humanity. Through him all the Father's blessings flow, and all our prayers are presented to the Father. All other priesthood comes from and shares in the priesthood of Christ. (1544f.)

The whole body of the faithful is also considered to share in his priesthood. Through their baptism they too have the task of proclaiming the truth of the gospel and the sanctification of all creation. Therefore the Church speaks of the *priesthood of the laity, or of all believers*. This, however, is not the same as the ministerial priesthood of orders, which exists to serve and sustain the common priesthood of all believers. (1547)

Through the ordained priesthood, bishops, priests and deacons represent the person of Christ to the whole community, proclaiming his Word, administering the sacraments and bringing his Eucharistic presence to the people in the Mass. (1554)

Bishops, being the successors of the apostles, are said to have 'the fullness of the priesthood'. At ordination (formerly called consecration) the bishop is given the authority to act as a representative of Christ as teacher, shepherd and priest. (1555)

Priests, the second rank in the hierarchy, act as vicars of the bishop, working with him and under his authority. In their parishes they represent the local bishop. (1562ff.)

Deacons, the third rank in the order of priesthood, are ordained to assist the bishop and the priests in proclaiming Christ's teaching and administering some sacraments, but they do not have the power to consecrate the Eucharist or absolve from sin. Since Vatican II, the diaconate, rather than being considered merely as a stepping-stone to the priesthood, is now also recognized as a separate and permanent ministry, to which, unlike the priesthood, married men can be admitted. (1571)

In the Latin Church, the orders of bishop and priest are normally reserved to those who undertake lifelong celibacy, although recently there have been exceptions to this. Some married Anglican clergy, having become Catholic, have been admitted to the Catholic priesthood.

In the Catholic Church, too, the sacrament of holy orders is conferred exclusively on men and only by a bishop, which stresses the apostolic succession.

(Note: A letter of Pope John Paul II in May 1994, after the publication of the Catechism, effectively rules out the possibility of the ordination of women to priesthood in the Roman Catholic Church in the foreseeable future.)

Q.54 Is not marriage something very special between two people? So why should the Church be involved in such a private matter?

A. Marriage is the love-based vocation to which most people are called. The Catechism says that God created marriage when he created the first humans and gave them as equals, to one another. This holiest of unions is so intimate that 'two become one flesh' and are united until death (and not, as the Catechism points out in a rare flash of humour, 'until further notice'). (1603ff., 1646)

Marriage is a most precious and personal matter. But it is much more. The Catechism tells us that Christ's presence at the marriage feast at Cana raised marriage to the dignity of a sacrament and was 'a proclamation that henceforth marriage would be a sacramental sign of his presence' with the married couple. (1613)

Since the Church is the custodian of all the sacraments, she is concerned to protect and sanctify the sacramental union in marriage.

Because of our fallen nature (cf. original sin), we are always prone to error and sin, even within marriage. Therefore sacramental grace should be available to married couples as a safeguard and protection of their relationship with each other and also with any children they may have.

In St Matthew's Gospel, Jesus explained that God willed that marriage should be permanent; the permission given by Moses to divorce was simply a concession to 'the hardness of heart' of the people of that time. Jesus added 'What therefore God has joined together, let no man put asunder' (Matt 19:3–9). (1615)

The Catechism adds that by its nature, the institution of marriage and married love is ordered to the good of the couple themselves and to the procreation and education of children and that, in them, it finds its crowning glory. The family that is blessed with children, becomes, in a real sense, a little church in its own right. In this 'domestic church' the children will receive the first instruction in the faith. The family church is a 'community of grace and prayer, a school of human virtues and of Christian charity'. (1638, 1655ff., 1666)

Married life is such an intimate sharing that, as the Catechism says, it can transform selfishness to self-giving. This does not guarantee there will not be difficulties. There always are, in any marriage, even the most perfect. It is for this reason that the grace of the sacrament is so necessary and valuable.

Every sacrament has a minister, usually a member of the clergy. Marriage, however, is unique in that the couple themselves, when they exchange vows, act as the ministers of the sacrament to one another. The 'officiating' cleric at that point is no more than an essential official witness, together with the bridesmaid and the best man. (1623)

The marriage of Catholics is often celebrated during a Nuptial Mass. This has the advantage of allowing the bride and groom to seal their union in the most solemn of settings, of receiving Holy Communion together and of having the Eucharistic Christ as a guest at their wedding. (1621)

Some married couples cannot have children. The Catechism says they have 'a conjugal life, full of meaning, in human and Christian terms. Their marriage can radiate a fruitfulness of charity, of hospitality and of sacrifice.' (1654)

There are those, also, who spend their lives as single people. Theirs is an equally special and important vocation. (1658)

Does not the Church ever allow separation or even divorce in certain circumstances? The Catechism admits that there are some situations in which continuing to live together becomes practically impossible for a variety of reasons. If efforts at reconciliation fail, then the Church accepts that the couple may have to live apart. However, as they remain married in the eyes of the Church they cannot remarry. (Sometimes such couples may have recourse to civil divorce. Vatican II says that the Church must be compassionate in such cases, especially where one party is innocent and does not wish to remarry. People in this situation are of course in no way barred from Holy Communion.) (1648ff.)

There are instances where, after careful examination, it is found that for some reason (failure to understand the real nature of marriage, or sexual impotence, or immaturity, or because one of the parties was not in fact free to marry, being already married or being in holy orders and not dispensed from them) an apparent marriage was not in fact a marriage at all. In such cases the Church can issue a decree of nullity. This, however, is not a dissolution of marriage but rather a solemn, legal statement that, despite appearances, in this case no marriage actually existed and those involved therefore are free to marry. Decrees of nullity are normally granted only after meticulous and sometimes lengthy consideration by the ecclesiastical courts. This is to ensure that in cases where a true marriage did, in fact, exist, that marriage should not be endangered.

PART THREE

LIFE IN CHRIST

Q.55 What must we do to be truly happy?

A. Probably there is no other question asked so often by so many. We want to be happy. It is a desire put into every human heart by God himself to draw us to him. We cannot be happy without him. So, the only way to achieve happiness truly and fully is by following his laws, seeing him as the end of all that we do. He has made each one of us for himself. As St Augustine wrote, and as the Catechism quotes: 'Our hearts are restless until they rest in thee.' (1718f.)

But, to achieve this happiness and the joy that comes with it, we have to purify our hearts from any desire contrary to God's commands. This is a constant struggle. We want to be good, but because of original sin, we are often attracted to what is evil, the flesh constantly struggling against the spirit.

The way to true happiness is outlined in Jesus' Sermon on the Mount, in the Beatitudes, so called because in Latin each statement begins with the word *Beati*, meaning both 'blessed' and 'happy'. Here they are:

> Blessed are the poor in spirit, for theirs is the Kingdom of heaven.
> Blessed are they who mourn, for they shall be comforted.
> Blessed are the meek, for they shall inherit the earth.
> Blessed are those who hunger and thirst for righteousness, for they shall be satisfied.
> Blessed are the merciful, for they shall obtain mercy.
> Blessed are the pure of heart, for they shall see God.
> Blessed are the peacemakers, for they shall be called the children of God.
> Blessed are those who are persecuted for the sake of righteousness, for theirs is the Kingdom of heaven.
> Blessed are you when you are reviled and persecuted and when people speak all kinds of evil against you falsely on my account. Rejoice and be glad, for your reward is great in heaven. (Matt 5:3–12)

Many of these situations, which Jesus promises will bring happiness, are quite contrary to our human ideas. We tend to believe that we are better off without these kinds of difficulties, trouble and struggles. Happiness, for most of us, is generally equated with a comfortable life and at least sufficient money. But in the sermon, Jesus shows that true happiness and fulfilment come from our doing our best to create a just society. He does not demand that we achieve this aim. His promise of happiness is made to all those who simply do their best to work for the establishment of God's Kingdom of justice, love and peace. (1723)

Q.56 How much freedom do people truly have in the way they behave, especially as the Church teaches that our freedom was restricted by the sin of the first human beings?

A. Every person has been given the freedom by God to decide whether to choose good or evil. This freedom is one of the ways in which we are made in the likeness of God and it is the gift that makes us different from the rest of creation. By our intelligence and will we are able to work out what we should do or say on any particular occasion. The phrase in the Our Father, 'and lead us not into temptation' (better phrased, perhaps, as 'and do not let us yield to temptation'), indicates that we do have free choice between sin and sanctity, good and evil. Because we have this ability we are also responsible for shaping our own lives. It is true that this freedom was limited by the sin of Adam and Eve, who abused their freedom and disobeyed God. But this did not destroy our freedom to choose what is right, and God continues to guide us in that choice. He also sent his only Son to die and rise from the dead to end the slavery of sin and lead us to ultimate freedom by his teaching and by the gift of the Holy Spirit. (1732ff., 1739ff.)

Some may argue that we cannot be truly free if we are subject to the moral law. But, paradoxically, we only become truly free by sticking to the law. Choosing good increases our freedom. The more we pray to God and the more we listen to and accept the promptings of his grace, the greater our inner freedom becomes, and the stronger we become in facing the pressures and problems of life. Choosing evil or what is wrong only helps to enslave us to selfishness and sin, and may even lead to a habit of sin which can be very difficult to break. As St Matthew reminds us, in his gospel, no one can serve two masters (Matt 6:24).

However, certain considerations can lessen our responsibility for our actions. These include ignorance that our behaviour is wrong (such as not knowing a particular traffic law and therefore breaking it) or being under duress or enslaved by a particular habit. Also we cannot be held fully responsible for a bad action if we could not reasonably have foreseen that it might happen. This would be the case if we lost our own lives in an attempt to help someone in serious danger. It would not however apply if a drunken driver killed someone. In this case the person would be guilty of serious sin if they deliberately became drunk, knowing that drunken driving often kills. (1735)

Individual rights to freedom are God-given and should always be respected. Civil authorities are responsible for ensuring this, especially in matters of morality and religion. We all have the right to our religious beliefs and practice. Our right to freedom, however, does not mean we can always say or do just as we wish. None of us is self-sufficient. We live in a community and we must always weigh up against the good of others what we intend to do or say. As St John says in his first letter, 'How can we love the God we cannot see if we do not love the brother or sister we do see?' (1 John 4:20). (1738, 2840)

The primacy of conscience does not mean that we can always do or say just as we wish. Our actions and words must be based on an informed conscience and on an awareness of Christian teaching. (1783ff.)

Q.57 How can we know the difference between right and wrong? Are some things always wrong no matter how good our intention?

A. As we have seen, God created each of us with free will and therefore we are responsible for our behaviour (unless we are in extraordinary circumstances, for example where the balance of reason has been weakened or lost). In every action that we decide to take, three elements should be considered: the *object* or what we are aiming to achieve, the *intention* behind what we do, and the *circumstances* that we are in. (1750)

For any act to be good the object must be good, so must the intention. Even a good intention cannot make wrong behaviour right. We may never do wrong so that good may come out of it. For instance, deliberate and serious lying, even to protect someone's reputation, is always wrong. On the other hand, an intention such as to earn praise by giving ostentatiously to charity is wrong even though the object itself obviously is not. (1753)

We should always act towards others as we would wish them to act towards us; the Catechism calls this 'the Golden Rule'. (1789)

The degree of guilt for any wrongdoing can be altered by the circumstances. For example, doing something wrong under the threat of serious violence or even death. However, some actions are always objectively wrong no matter what the intention or circumstances. These include murder, adultery, perjury, blasphemy and sex outside marriage. (1756)

Our responsibility for choosing between right and wrong depends on our conscience. This small guiding voice deep within our being is not a human voice that we can actually hear, but a prompting and guidance that we sense in making our judgement. It comes from God himself. Only by following a well-formed conscience can we have true peace of heart and mind. (1776ff.)

An enlightened conscience constantly directs us towards the good and away from evil, and we must train ourselves to listen to it. This can be a lifetime's work. It can happen that a person acts wrongly because their conscience is not properly formed. Obviously this can lessen any blame, especially if the ignorance is due to bad example or lack of knowledge of Christ's teaching. In some cases the person may not be guilty at all even though their action is objectively evil. But if the ignorance is because there has been little effort to discover the truth or to develop the conscience, then guilt remains. (1784, 1793)

Sometimes it can be difficult to know the difference between right and wrong. In these cases advice should be sought from people who can truly and wisely help us. Also, the Holy Spirit should be asked for guidance.

All human beings have a right and duty to follow their conscience in the way they judge correct. No one should be forced to act against their conscience. Civil authorities are responsible for creating conditions where this is possible, especially in the belief and practice of religion. (1738)

Q.58 What are virtues? How can a person become virtuous?

A. Calling a person 'virtuous' nowadays is not necessarily a compliment. It can mean that they are not much fun and are not prepared to 'enjoy life'. The opposite is the case. Virtuous people are joyful and happy and in control of themselves and their passions. In fact, the word 'virtue' refers to anything that helps us make the best of ourselves and our talents and direct our lives towards what is good. (1803)

Like so much that is worthwhile in life it is not an easy task to become virtuous, but we can achieve it by hard work and practice. The more we try, the better we become. We can also call constantly on God's grace through prayer and the sacraments. (1804ff.)

The central (also known as cardinal) virtues in daily life are prudence, justice, fortitude and temperance.

Prudence means that we look where we are going in life, trying to find and follow the right direction. It also helps us to listen to and follow the guidance of our conscience. (1806)

Justice helps us recognize and accept all that we owe to God and neighbour. (1807)

Fortitude gives us the strength to stick to our principles in temptation and always to follow our Christian faith, even under threat of death. (1808)

Through temperance we are able to control all our passions and desires. We control them rather than allow them to control us. (1809)

Apart from these cardinal virtues, there are also what are known as the theological virtues: faith, hope and charity. The greatest of these is charity, more commonly known as love. The Scriptures tell us that this is the virtue that will last beyond all others. It is the virtue which enables us to love God and all other human beings for his sake. It can never die, and it is the only one that will be with us in the next life. We have some rather restricted ideas about love nowadays, often looking at it from a selfish or sexual point of view. But genuine love has no connection with selfishness. It only wants the good of the other at all costs. (1813, 1822ff.)

Faith enables us to believe in God, all that he has taught us and all that the Church teaches. However, believing is not enough. For faith to be living it must be the source of good works and help us to carry out Christ's teaching. Those who have received the gift of faith must also be prepared to defend it even if it means death. (1814ff.)

If we possess the virtue of hope we are able to put our trust in all of Christ's promises. We know we cannot achieve this by our own power but only with God's help. To lead a virtuous and genuinely Christian life we also need the support of the Holy Spirit's grace and gifts. These are wisdom, understanding, counsel, fortitude, knowledge, piety and fear of the Lord. (1817, 1830ff.)

Q.59 What is sin?

A. Sin is any action, word, thought or lack of action that is contrary to the genuine love of God, our neighbour or ourselves. It breaks the natural law which is deep in our hearts and it turns us away from God and his love, making us self-centred rather than God-centred. Every human being sins (with the exception of Mary, the Mother of God), and if we say we have no sin we are fooling ourselves. But if we admit our sin, are genuinely sorry, resolve to try not to make the same mistake again, and ask God's forgiveness, we will receive it. God's mercy is without limit if we are ready to forgive others in our turn. The Lord's Prayer reminds us: 'Forgive us our trespasses as we forgive those who trespass against us.' God showed us just how great his mercy is when he sent his only Son to die for us and, by his sacrifice, save us from our sins and restore our friendship with him. (1849ff.)

Many kinds of sin are mentioned in Scripture. In the Catechism, they are dealt with in the section on the Ten Commandments. Breaking or acting contrary to one of these God-given laws is always sinful to a greater or lesser degree.

The Church has always taught that there are two main categories of sin: mortal, which is extremely serious and destroys the life of grace in the soul, and venial, which weakens that life. For a sin to be truly mortal, three conditions must be fulfilled: the act must be grave, the sin must be committed with full knowledge of how wrong it is, and with full and free consent to go ahead in spite of this. Grave matter includes the sins listed in the Ten Commandments, such as blasphemy, murder and adultery. However, the seriousness of any sin can be diminished if the person genuinely does not know how wrong it is or if they are swayed by strong passions or acting under pressure. If full consent and full knowledge are lacking, even if the matter is grave, the sin would only be venial. Mortal sin, on the other hand, is so serious that it must be forgiven in the sacrament of reconciliation wherever possible, and there must be genuine repentance and intention, with God's grace, not to repeat it. Unforgiven or unrepented mortal sins incur the eternal death of hell. Nevertheless, the Catechism reminds us that, in the end, each person is subject to the great justice and the infinite mercy of God. Although the Church has taught that many people, such as the saints, are in heaven, it has never taught that any one individual is definitely in hell. (1854ff.)

Although venial sins are less serious than mortal, because the action is not grave, constantly committing them weakens the grace of God in our souls and can lead to mortal sin. They can also cloud our conscience and make it more difficult to decide between right and wrong. (1862f.)

Some sins are also known as vices or capital sins because they give rise to a variety of further wrongdoing. These are pride, avarice, envy, anger, lust, gluttony and sloth.

Although sin is essentially something we commit personally, we also share responsibility for the sins of others if we directly co-operate with them, if we praise or protect them, or do not try, where possible, to prevent them from sinning. It is also possible that society can create structures that are sinful (such as apartheid) which lead to more sin. (1869)

Q.60 Can a person be a Christian in isolation?

A. Christ's teaching is all about relationship and love: first with God, whom we must love above all else, and then with all other human beings, 'our neighbours'. People were not made to be selfish, but to share themselves, their talents, knowledge and possessions. As we are asked in the gospels, if we do not show that we care for and genuinely love our brother or sister whom we can see, how can we claim to love God, whom we cannot see? True faith must be visible in the way we behave towards others. Understanding the importance of this inter-dependence is increasing and spreading throughout the whole world as we realize what it means to be brothers and sisters, equal in the sight of God and responsible for each other and our planet. In recognizing this interdependence, in a small way we are echoing the inseparability of the community of the Trinity; the relationship of three persons in one God.

From the beginning, men and women were created to live in community and, acting together, they can achieve far more than any one individual. Living and working in society, we develop our human potential. We should also see that the society in which we live develops justly. The purpose of any particular society is to secure the good of every individual, especially of those who are not able to care for themselves, and to work for the common good. In drawing up its laws, the State must respect the dignity of each one and encourage people to fulfil themselves, to take responsibility for their own actions and to look after those in their immediate care, such as members of their own family. (1905ff.)

No society can function properly without someone in charge, and the authority of governments and others in power comes from God and they should be obeyed as far as their demands are just. It is possible that those in power may misuse their authority and act against the moral law or the common good. Those who realize this and are able to do something about changing it for the better have a duty to do so. (1902f., 2238)

Q.61 What are the responsibilities of Christians in public life?

A. All Christians are called to help to develop a just society, a community that recognizes all human beings have equal dignity and right to respect because they are children of the one God, created in his image. We are also all equal because each one of us is redeemed by the sacrifice of Christ and is called to share eternal happiness with God in heaven. (1929ff.)

A just society can be recognized by the way it encourages all groups and individuals, especially the disadvantaged, to enjoy full human rights and all that is due to them, materially and spiritually. World peace depends upon this. Any discrimination, whether sexual or racial, is against Christ's teaching. Ending such injustice cannot be achieved simply by legislation, but only by people recognizing in their hearts that all are brothers and sisters. This is not happening at the moment and the Catechism points out that millions of people suffer from 'sinful inequalities' which are totally against Christ's teaching. (1935, 1938)

People need people. God has given each of us different talents and virtues. They are not distributed equally, but by sharing with each other we help to create a healthy society. Together we can do more than any one of us can do alone. The Catechism uses the word 'solidarity', which means co-operation between people on all sorts of levels, such as between employers and employees and between rich and poor. Such an attitude should help to create an atmosphere where any dispute can be settled by negotiation and discussion rather than by violence. (1937, 1939)

A just society can only be created when each individual recognizes that every neighbour is 'another self'. There is no exception to this and it particularly applies to the weak and disadvantaged. It even includes all our enemies and those who would do us evil or harm us. Even though we must hate any sin, we should love the sinner and where possible try to help them. The Catechism reminds us of the saying of Jesus, 'As you did it to the least of these my brethren you did it to me' (Matt 25:40).

Any society that refuses to recognize the equality of all undermines its own authority and endangers peace. Although the Church does not generally involve itself in politics, if the State flouts the basic laws of justice the Church has a duty to step in and remind people of their obligations. Over the centuries Christian men and women have worked to end discrimination and promote justice, liberating slaves, healing the sick, communicating the liberation and equality preached by Christianity and doing all possible to create conditions which permit people throughout the world to live a dignified life worthy of a human being. (1942)

Q.62 What is the moral law?

A. Law may seem a strange concept to include when we are discussing a religion based on love. But it is only through keeping the moral law, God's guidance for human happiness, that we are able to avoid evil and find true fulfilment, live a life of love and reach our eternal destiny. As we have seen, human beings are essentially social beings. None of us can do exactly as we wish all the time. We have to follow some system of law if we are to serve the common good and survive as a community. (1950)

The moral law is expressed in a variety of ways, all related: eternal law, which is the source of all law, natural law, as revealed in the Bible, and civil and church law. The natural law is not something outside us, it is written on our hearts by the creator, and is based on the fundamental desire for God experienced by all human beings whether or not they follow any religion. It is possible to come to know it by human reason. No one is free to ignore this law no matter what their background or culture, and it can never be destroyed. However, although this law is natural it is not always immediately obvious to everyone. Because of our sinful condition we have to make some effort to work it out. (1954ff.)

The first stage of the revelation of the natural law is found in the Old Testament where God chooses Israel as his people and gives the law to Moses. It sets out common principles to help the community survive and it is summed up in the Ten Commandments, which remain the basis of much civil law today. Everything that is contrary to the love of God and of our neighbour is forbidden. These laws protect us against the ever present attraction of evil. But at this early, biblical stage, knowledge of the natural law is not complete. It prepares us for the 'new law' which we find in the life and teaching of Jesus. His law of perfect love is summed up in the Sermon on the Mount which sets out the ideal way of Christian life. Much of it turns our practical way of thinking on its head by praising the sort of people we often think should be pitied, such as the humble and the persecuted. It sets out to reform and purify the human heart, the origin of all our choices, good or bad, and urges us to work for a better world, the world of the Kingdom of God. 'The new law of Jesus is to love each other as he loved us.' It is called a law of love because it makes us act from love, not from fear. It sets us free. (1961ff., 1965ff.)

Q.63 What does holiness mean? Can anyone become holy?

A. Holy is another word for perfect and God calls everyone to achieve this state. Jesus put it in very few words: 'Be perfect as your heavenly

Father is perfect' (Matt 5:48). It is one of the toughest demands in the gospels, but one for which God offers a great deal of help and strength if we are prepared to accept it. St John Chrysostom is quoted in the Catechism as saying 'Our virtue does not depend on our work alone but on grace from on high'. Holiness grows in us the more we try to live out God's commandments, love him and our neighbour and turn to him in prayer, which helps us to see what his purpose for us is. (2013ff.)

God's help for living the virtuous life is freely given to us and helps to turn our minds and hearts towards him and his will. It is a free gift and we are free to accept it or not. How and why God chooses to give this grace is a mystery.

The Church teaches that various kinds of grace are given at different times. Sacraments for example are all channels of grace when received worthily. The initial experience of grace comes in baptism. This fills the soul with what is known as 'sanctifying' grace, bringing the Holy Spirit to live in our souls, healing sin, both original and personal, and setting us off on the lifelong journey towards eternal life. We are said to be justified, or filled with God's grace. This happy state is not earned by our own merit, but by the sacrifice of Jesus, which won for us the reward of eternal life. This is also called being in a 'state of grace', and it helps us to live according to God's will. Only through mortal sin can this grace be destroyed, although even then it can be restored by genuine repentance and in the sacrament of reconciliation. (1992, 2000, 2023)

Another form of grace is 'actual grace', which is given by God when and as he judges, to help us at various times in our lives. There are also special graces, sometimes known as 'charisms', which include extraordinary gifts such as speaking in tongues. These graces are given to certain individuals to help the whole Church grow in holiness. All Christian vocations too, such as preaching and teaching, have particular graces.

Since grace is essentially part of supernatural life, the life of our souls, we cannot really know, except by faith, whether we possess it or not. However, Scripture tells us that we can judge someone's degree of holiness or grace by their actions: 'By their fruits you shall know them.' The Pope in his introduction to the Catechism says (quoting James 2:17) 'If faith is not expressed in works, it is dead'. The Catechism also includes a thought-provoking quote from St Joan of Arc. When asked by hostile ecclesiastical judges whether she was in a state of God's grace, she replied 'If I am not, may it please God to put me in it; if I am, may it please God to keep me there'.

Our relationship with God begins with a gift of his grace, which is not merited by us. As our relationship deepens through prayer with the help of the Holy Spirit we grow in grace and good works and can bring grace to others. But becoming holy is never easy and cannot be achieved without constant self-denial, spiritual struggle and regular prayer. However, Christians are inspired by the hope that with God's grace they will be able to persevere in this struggle until death and enter eternal life with God.

Q.64 What are the 'precepts' of the Church? Why are such rules necessary?

A. Although the Church is founded on Christ, God made man, it is run and organized by human beings and, like any other human organization, requires rules. These rules in the case of the Catholic Church are called precepts and they are designed to help people both develop a prayer life and grow in loving others by fulfilling at least the minimum duties in their life and worship. They are all positive commands and state that all Catholics shall:

1 Attend Mass on Sundays.
2 Receive the sacrament of reconciliation at least once a year if conscious of any grave sin. This is in order to receive the sacrament of Holy Communion worthily.
3 Receive Holy Communion at least once a year some time during the Easter season: the very minimum required of someone who wishes to be part of the Catholic community.
4 Attend Mass on all holy days of obligation. This means on all the principal feasts: Christmas, Epiphany, Ascension Day, Corpus Christi, Sts Peter and Paul, the Assumption, the Feast of All Saints and, in some countries, the Feast of Our Lady's Immaculate Conception. Sometimes the feasts are transferred to the nearest Sunday or, as in the case of the Feast of St Joseph, are no longer holy days of obligation. Bishops have the power, however, to decide in their own

diocese which holy days should be kept.

5 Keep all the days set aside for fasting (only taking one full meal) and abstinence (not eating meat). At one time, every Friday was a day of abstinence from meat. This is no longer the case but it has been replaced with a call to mark every Friday with some form of self-denial in memory of the death of Jesus. Currently only Ash Wednesday, at the beginning of Lent, and Good Friday are days of both fasting and abstinence. The discipline of denying oneself food and practising penance is to help us develop our spiritual natures and free ourselves from selfishness. It is common to all great religions.

6 All members of the Church have a duty to give as much as they can afford to help support their parish and clergy. (2042)

Q.65 What are the Ten Commandments and how do they relate to modern living?

A. The Ten Commandments are God's own instructions on how people should live. They set out what is right and wrong for any civilized society and apply to every human being always. Because of this, the Church teaches that they are 'written on the heart of every man and woman'. They are also regarded as part of the 'natural law', because it is believed that even if a person has not been taught what they are, he or she can become aware of them through human reasoning. It is because they are such an essential part of human civilization that they apply in every age. Although these laws are carried in the human heart, they were set out in words by God because original sin had dimmed human nature and its ability to recognize the moral law. (2070)

Tradition teaches that these commandments were given by God to Moses as he led the Israelites out of slavery in Egypt towards the land that God had promised them. The commandments, which are also known as the Decalogue, which simply means 'ten words', are believed to have been engraved on two tablets of stone and carried with great reverence by the Israelites in a portable shrine, the Ark of the Covenant, until eventually they were placed in the Temple in Jerusalem.

They cover every aspect of human relationships with God and all his creation. All ten are closely linked, because they are all based on our love of God and love of neighbour that stems from that. Consequently the Church teaches that to break one is in some way to go against them all. (2069)

The commandments are in two sections. The first contains the three relating to God and our duties to him, and the second group deal with our neighbour.

1 I am the Lord your God who brought you out of the land of Egypt, out of the house of bondage. You shall have no other gods before me.
2 You shall not take the name of the Lord your God in vain.
3 Remember to keep holy the Lord's Day.
4 Honour your father and mother.
5 You shall not kill.
6 You shall not commit adultery.
7 You shall not steal.
8 You shall not bear false witness against your neighbour.
9 You shall not covet your neighbour's wife.
10 You shall not covet your neighbour's goods.

Christ, who introduced the new law, did not replace the commandments but developed and strengthened them. The gospels tell the story of the rich young man who asked Jesus how he could reach eternal life. Jesus tells him he must keep all the commandments. Only then could he have the possibility of greater perfection by giving up his wealth and following Jesus, which, as the story tells us, the young man felt unable to do.

Jesus also gave a stricter interpretation of the commandments than they previously had. For example, he taught that 'it was said of old that you shall not kill, but I say that everyone who is angry with his brother is liable to judgement'. He also told his disciples to turn the other cheek if they were attacked and to go so far as even to love their enemies.

The list of commandments may seem to reduce religion to a series of rules and regulations, and rather negative ones at that. However, the Catechism reminds us that they are essentially about love. When Jesus was asked which of the commandments was the greatest, he said 'You shall love the Lord your God with all your heart, and with all your soul, and with all your mind. This is the greatest and first commandment. And the second is like it: you shall love your neighbour as yourself. On these two commandments hang all the law and the prophets'

(Matt 22:37–40). The commandments are not intended to restr
human freedom but to free us to be truly human. (2054f.)

Q.66 The first commandment seems to apply essentially to the Israelites of the time of Moses. How does it apply today?

A. This commandment is the foundation of all the commandments a
sums up the main purpose of human life: to worship the one true G
and love him above all. The full text reads 'I am the Lord your Go
who brought you out of the land of Egypt, out of the house of bondag
You shall have no other gods before me. You shall not make for yourse.
a graven image, or any likeness of anything that is in heaven above, o.
that is in the earth beneath, or that is in the water under the earth; you
shall not bow down to them or serve them.'

This teaching is the basis of three great world religions, in order of
foundation, Judaism, Christianity and Islam, all of which worship the
one God, the God of Abraham, Isaac and Jacob. (2085)

By God we mean the Creator, Saviour and Master of all that is, a
being of infinite and merciful love who does not and never will change.
(2086)

The Catechism teaches that all evil stems from our neglecting our
relationship with God, and says that every human being has the
responsibility 'to seek the truth, especially in what concerns God and
his Church, and to embrace it and hold on to it as they come to know
it'. This duty is rooted in the very dignity of the human person. It is
only by putting God first in our lives that we can be freed from the
slavery of selfishness and sin. The reference to the Church is not to
discriminate against non-Christian religions, which also 'can reflect a
ray of truth that enlightens all'. (2104)

We all have a duty to adore the God who created us and we do this
first in prayer both as individuals and in community. This is essential
if we are to keep God's commandments. We must also protect our faith
in God by rejecting everything that conflicts with it. This includes
doubting what God has revealed, or flatly refusing to believe it. Other
sins against the commandment are heresy, apostasy and schism. Heresy
is the denial by a baptized person of any truth that is part of the faith,
taught with certainty by the Catholic Church; apostasy is completely

rejecting Christian faith after baptism; and schism is the refusal of sub-mission to the Pope or of communion with Christians in communion with him. The first commandment also forbids despair, i.e. believing that it is impossible for God to save us, and presumption, i.e. believing that we will be saved no matter what we do. (2089)

It is important to consider the context of this commandment, which came at a time when the tribes of the Middle East worshipped a great variety of gods and goddesses. Modern society does not have idols of that kind, but there are many other 'false gods' that are often put before God the creator, such as money, power, sex and even extreme nationalism.

Q.67 If the first commandment forbids making 'graven images' why do Catholic churches contain so many statues and other images?

A. This commandment forbids the worship of idols. That means put-ting anything in the place of God and adoring it, believing that such an object can do what only God can, either answer our prayers and peti-tions or in any way influence our lives.

Catholics do not worship statues or give them the honour that is due to God alone. Images simply represent Mary the mother of God or the saints, and are displayed in churches in order to encourage others to follow their example. People do pray before these images but only to honour those whom they represent for the way they dedicated their lives to the love and service of God. The saints are never seen as replacements for God, but can be asked to intercede with him on our behalf. (2132)

This is especially true of the Virgin Mary who as mother of Jesus, God made man, has a special role in bringing our needs to God. There are a vast number of representations of Mary in Catholic churches, but devotion to her is simply devotion to another human being; she is never regarded as being divine. (971)

Even in Old Testament times certain images were permitted that in some way symbolized God's promise of salvation, and the Seventh Council of Nicaea, in 787, justified the use of icons, holy representa-tions of Jesus, his mother and the saints, by teaching that Jesus, in becoming a human person, had shown in himself an image of God, and so introduced a new idea of, and purpose for, sacred images. (1160f., 2141)

Q.68 What is forbidden by the first commandment? Are horoscopes included, as some newspapers have reported?

A. Anyone who deliberately rejects God, or who claims to put their faith in other supernatural powers, breaks this commandment. To take horoscopes seriously is forbidden because those who produce them claim the power to see into the future, and also that people's lives and free will can be controlled by outside influences, namely the stars. Only God can know the future and has indeed revealed it on occasion to some of the prophets and saints. All 'unhealthy curiosity about the future' such as palm reading and interpreting omens is also forbidden by this commandment, as is any attempt to contact the dead through mediums and any involvement in the occult, especially black magic or Satanism, even if such involvement should arise from a desire to heal or cure. All superstition is also forbidden, including the belief that simply reciting the words of certain prayers will achieve automatic results. (2116f.)

Other offences against this commandment are sacrilege, the treating of the sacraments and other holy objects unworthily, and simony, buying and selling spiritual things. (2120ff.)

The Catechism says that one of the most serious problems of today is atheism, the denial of God's existence. Atheists see human life as an end in itself and believe they are totally in charge of their own destiny. Sometimes those who do believe in God can be partly to blame for people being atheists if they give a bad example or a wrong impression of the true nature of God and his teaching. The Catechism points out that such behaviour must be said to conceal God, rather than to reveal him. Agnosticism, the claim that it is not possible to know whether or not God exists, is also against this commandment. The Catechism however points out that, in some cases, those who call themselves agnostics may well be simply searching for God. (2123ff.)

Q.69 What does 'taking the name of the Lord in vain' mean, and what is its importance today?

A. This commandment is perhaps one of those most ignored today. It forbids any use of the name of God, Father, Son or Spirit, or that of any holy person or thing irreverently or as a swear word. These names should always be respected and only used in prayer. Sometimes, however, when people exclaim 'Oh God!' or use the Holy Name or the phrase 'Jesus, Mary and Joseph' it is more a prayer than an insult. They are calling for help. Some of the psalms, too, may seem as though they are complaining or railing against God. This is not to misuse his name. It is a human being crying out to the creator, perhaps in puzzlement or pain, much as a child might cry to its parents. It is a use of God's name based on faith and trust. (2144)

One of the most serious offences against this commandment is blasphemy; using any words of hatred or defiance against God, his Church or any holy person or thing. This is always evil. Blasphemy is also an offence in the laws of many nations. The importance of the second commandment is also shown by the fact that it is the basis of the structure of most Western law. Everyone appearing in a court of law is normally required to swear before Almighty God to tell the truth, the whole truth and nothing but the truth. (Those who claim to have no faith are not required to take the oath, but are required to 'attest', which is a solemn undertaking to tell the truth.) Lying in these circumstances is perjury and is both a sin against this commandment and a crime in law. (2148, 2152)

Other offences against this commandment include breaking a promise made under oath. However, anyone has the right to refuse to take an oath if to do so would offend against human dignity or church teaching. (2155)

Q.70 What does the third commandment mean by keeping the Sabbath Day holy? Is all work forbidden?

A. This commandment centres around the need of all human beings to set aside time and space for God and for re-creation for themselves. This is done by taking a break from daily work and the concerns of material life or, as the Catechism puts it, 'worship of money'. This one day, different from the rest, is also described as a protest against 'the servitude of work'. (2176)

The Sabbath is holy for various reasons. The Bible says that on the seventh day (the Sabbath) God rested from his work of creating the universe and all that is in it. If God took a rest, human beings should be able to follow this example! For Christians, the Jewish Sabbath has been replaced by the Sunday, marking the day of the week when Jesus rose from the dead. Because this event brought in new creation, it has become the first of all days, the Lord's Day. (2175)

Christians are expected to celebrate Sunday by worshipping God, recognizing his goodness. Sharing in prayer is the most important way of doing this as it helps us strengthen each other. The Sunday Eucharist or the Mass is at the heart of community prayer. It dates back to the time of the apostles, and has always been central to Christian faith. Mother Teresa has said that without her daily Mass she could not continue to carry out her work. Because of the unique importance of the Eucharist and the great benefits that it brings, the Church continues to consider it a grave sin for Catholics deliberately to miss Mass on Sunday and holy days of obligation unless there are important reasons, such as sickness, or the need to look after small children. (2181)

In many parts of the world it is increasingly difficult for people to attend Mass, due to a shortage of priests. In these cases Catholics should try to come together to share in the Liturgy of the Word or in other joint prayers marking the Lord's Day. We also keep Sunday holy by finding time for silence and meditation and for helping others, especially the sick and elderly. (2184ff.)

Obviously certain kinds of work have to be done even on Sunday. These include providing essential public services, as in hospitals, and recreational activities, as in sports centres and restaurants. The Catechism says that those of us who are at leisure should not make unreasonable demands on those who have to work, and also that they should not be prevented from worshipping God. Christians are asked to do what they can to ensure that Sundays are kept as legal holidays and to defend the tradition of Sunday being a day apart, which has played an important role in the spiritual life of society. (2186)

Q.71 What are we asked to do by the fourth commandment?

A. The commandments are divided into two sections. The first deals with our relationship with God while the second sets out our duties and responsibilities to other people, our neighbours. These begin with this commandment, which deals with our most important relationship after God, that is with our parents. It is expanded in the Catechism to cover all family relationships and all dealings with those in any kind of authority. It is the only commandment that also tells of the benefits in this life when it is kept: peace and prosperity. Failing to keep it harms the whole community. (2197ff.)

The Christian family is seen as the 'domestic church' with all members equal in dignity and deserving of respect. It is the original cell of society, and it has been said that any community is only as strong and secure as the families in it. Respect for parents is a key part of Bible teaching because the fatherhood of God is seen as the basis of human parenthood. We should be grateful to our parents because they have helped to give us life and to develop as human beings. Children are obliged to obey their mother and father as long as they live at home. Even when they leave, they should still respect and support them, especially when they are old and infirm. (2204ff.)

The Catechism holds out an idealistic view of family life. It says that the normal family should consist of husband, wife and children, each of whom should help the others develop, in a home where there is always tenderness, forgiveness and mutual respect. It is in the love and security of the family that we first learn about every aspect of life: above all what it means to love and honour God, the difference between right and wrong, and how to play a full part in society.

Parents are responsible for educating their children in every way. The Catechism says it is impossible to overstate the importance of this. There can be no substitute. Parents are urged to give a good example as actions speak louder than words. Above all children must learn that spiritual development is more important than material success. Ways of assisting spiritual development include teaching children to pray, sharing daily family prayer and reading the Bible. Such a firm base will last a lifetime. When necessary parents should not be afraid to discipline a child.

In choosing a school, parents should see as far as possible that it continues the Christian education that has been started at home. When children grow up they have a right to decide how they will live and what job they will do. Parents can give advice but they must not use pressure. (2207ff., 2221, 2223)

The authorities in turn must see that parents are able to exercise their full rights and, as the family unit is so important to the whole society, they must also help to protect and strengthen it. Suitable housing, medical care and family benefits should be made available. Everything possible must also be done to protect young people from drugs, pornography and other damaging influences. When families are disadvantaged and unable to help themselves, they are entitled to State assistance.

In dealing with this commandment the Catechism gives a few lines for those who do not marry, perhaps in order to take care of their parents or other members of the family, or to devote themselves to a career. They too can contribute to the good of the whole human family. (2231, 2237)

Q.72 What are the Christian's responsibilities to the State? Must secular authorities always be obeyed even if their stand is against Christian teaching?

A. It is not enough for the Christian to restrict his or her concerns to family or intimate circles. Faith also demands that we work for a just society where all members are treated as equal, as they are in the sight of God. Everyone is bound to do all they can to build a community where there is justice and freedom for all, and especially for the disadvantaged and those who find it hard to look after themselves. Those in authority are reminded that they are servants of the people and are bound to work for justice and the common good. (2235ff.)

Those who have legitimate authority should be regarded as 'representatives of God who has made them stewards of his gifts'. However, Christians have a duty to speak out when they see authorities acting in a way that damages the dignity of people or the good of the community. (2238)

No person is obliged to obey demands or laws that are in conflict with the moral law, basic human rights, or the teachings of the gospel. Jesus said 'Render to Caesar the things that are Caesar's and to God the things that are God's'. However, all individuals are obliged to play a full part in society by paying just taxes, exercising the right to vote where available and defending their country under certain conditions. (2242)

Without belief in God, societies can easily become totalitarian, in which case the State tends to make unjust and immoral demands on the individual and on the family. (2244)

The Church claims the right to be involved in politics where there may be danger of an attack on human rights or where the salvation of souls is imperilled. At the wider, international level, richer countries have a responsibility towards the poorer. In international trade there is a constant danger of the exploitation of the weak by the strong, through disadvantageous trading conditions or unjust interest rates or conditions on loans.

When necessary, and as far as they can, States should welcome refugees from other countries and help them to find shelter and work. For their part, those who emigrate to any country, whether as refugees or for other legitimate reasons, are bound to respect the customs and laws of their host country. (1911)

Q.73 Is all killing forbidden by the fifth commandment?

A. The actual word used in the Bible for killing specifies that this commandment applies only to all innocent human beings. All killing therefore is not forbidden. Exceptions include self-defence, where causing death is not the primary intention. We all have a right, even a duty, to protect our lives and the lives of others, especially those of our families. The State also has the right to protect its citizens from crime by punishing criminals in a suitable way. As far as possible any punishment should help the offender to be rehabilitated. However if the crime is sufficiently serious it could even merit the death penalty, though the Catechism does not specify when this might be. But the general principle is that human life is sacred because God alone gives it. No one has the right to destroy an innocent person. (2261, 2263, 2266)

All murder is forbidden by this commandment as a sin 'that cries out to heaven for vengeance'. Also forbidden is any action intended to cause death, any refusal to help someone whose life is in danger or any action that puts our own lives or the lives of others at risk. (2268)

A serious sin against this commandment is abortion, 'a crime against human life' which damages the whole of society. (This is considered in Question 75.) Euthanasia or so-called mercy killing, whether voluntary or not, is always wrong no matter how good the intention. The weak, sick or handicapped deserve special respect and should be always helped to lead a life as normal as possible. However there is no obligation on medical staff to use extraordinary means of prolonging life. (2270ff., 2277ff.)

As health is a precious gift from God, we all have a duty to take care of it by avoiding anything that is damaging such as drugs, abuse of alcohol, food or tobacco. However, although we must take care of our bodies, we must not idolize physical perfection, putting it above all else. (2289)

Taking one's own life is always wrong, as life is a gift from God and is not ours to dispose of. However, the Catechism understands that there may well be states of mind such as anguish, severe depression or great suffering which can lessen the guilt of the person who commits suicide. We should not fear that those who do kill themselves will not be saved, as, in ways unknown to us, God can offer them repentance. (2280ff.)

All human beings must be helped to pass their last moments with dignity, and relatives of any dying person are responsible for seeing that they receive the last sacraments. Cremation is no longer against church teaching provided it is not carried out in order to deny the resurrection of the body. (2299)

Killing the body is not the only crime forbidden by this commandment. It also condemns damaging the life of grace in the soul by scandal. This means any behaviour that leads another person to sin. Jesus seldom criticized anyone, but of those who led others astray he said it was better if they had not been born. Scandal can also be given by those who create laws or social conditions that make it difficult to follow Christian teaching, and by anyone who uses a position of power to encourage others to do wrong. (2284ff.)

Q.74 Can war ever be justified?

A. The threat of war and the evils it brings constantly hangs over the world because of the presence of sin. Wars are caused by injustice, greed, envy and pride, and the Church calls on everyone to commit themselves to work for peace by doing all they can to help overcome such disorders. But it teaches that every country or State has the right to self-defence, even if this involves armed conflict. However, before war can be justified certain strict conditions must be fulfilled. These are: the damage inflicted by the aggressor must be grave and lasting; all other means than war must be tried and shown not to work; there should be serious prospect of success; and the use of arms must not cause greater evil than that which is to be destroyed. Whether these conditions are present should be decided by those responsible for the common good, normally the governments involved. They also have a right to call on citizens to join the various services necessary to defend their country. Those who feel unable to fight because this goes against their consciences should be prepared to help in some other way. (2308–2311)

Even if a just war is declared, certain actions remain immoral. Extermination of a whole nation or any ethnic minority is gravely sinful, and any attempt to destroy cities indiscriminately is a crime against God and humanity. Such destruction is sadly made ever more possible by the increasing sophistication of modern weapons. (2314)

In discussing the arms race, the Catechism says it may seem that the building up of weapons acts as a deterrent against war but in fact it achieves the opposite. The vast amount of money spent on arms is wrong because it deprives many people of essential food and shelter. (2315)

Other acts of war and aggression condemned by the Catechism are terrorism, all forms of torture, kidnapping or hostage taking. The Catechism recognizes that cruelty has been used by some governments while church pastors made no protest. It is now clear that these practices and the apparent condoning of them did not help keep public order, in fact only made matters worse. The Catechism asks us to pray for all those involved in such injustices. (2297, 2298)

Q.75 Why does the Church consider abortion such a serious sin?

A. Abortion has constantly been condemned by the Church since the first century. It has always taught that human life begins at the moment of conception, therefore the embryo must be given the full rights of any human person from that moment. The Catechism quotes from Vatican II: 'Life must be protected with the utmost care from the moment of conception: abortion and infanticide are abominable crimes.' (2271)

Anyone who has an abortion, or who is involved in the operation, freely and fully understanding the gravity of their action, is guilty of so serious a sin that they are automatically excommunicated from the Church; that is, officially cut off from the community and the sacraments. This is the only place in the Catechism where 'automatic' excommunication is mentioned. Such a serious punishment is not intended to show a lack of mercy, but to make clear the gravity of the action and the 'harm done to the innocent one who is put to death, to the parents and to the whole of society'. (2272)

Much is made today of what is known as 'the woman's right to choose' whether or not to have an abortion. The Catechism points out that no human being has the right to take an innocent life. The right to bestow or to take life belongs to God alone. (2273)

The Church also condemns any medical study on the embryo done with a view to abortion, and the production for medical research of human embryos which, on the completion of the experiment, may be destroyed. Likewise, all attempts to control the sex of a baby are contrary to human dignity. However, prenatal diagnosis which aims to safeguard or heal an embryo is perfectly acceptable. (2274f.)

The whole area of bioethics is developing so rapidly that there are individual questions not specifically tackled in the Catechism. However, the attitude of the Church is that any action that endangers or destroys human life, even at its earliest stages, is wrong and therefore forbidden.

Q.76 What does the Church teach about medical experimentation on human beings?

A. The Church fully recognizes that certain experiments, whether medical or psychological, can help those who are sick or suffering. It says that science is a precious gift, provided it is placed at the service of human beings and respects their human rights. Under these conditions, and if the individual concerned fully accepts all that is involved, the experiment may be justified. However, this can never be so if the proposed action is against the moral law or if it in any way puts a life in danger, even if the patient fully agrees to the operation. (2293)

Concerning organ transplants, the Catechism says these can be regarded as good if there is no disproportionate risk to the living donor. (Where the donor has died, it is important that the agreement of the next of kin be sought.) However, organ transplants can never be acceptable if those involved in the transfer, either donor or recipient, have not given their informed consent. Neither can they ever be permitted if someone is disabled or mutilated in order to provide an organ for another. (2296)

Q.77 What does the Church teach concerning the sixth commandment?

A. In creating men and women, male and female, God made them in his own image, and blessed them with the ability to give and receive love. He also made them equal to one another in dignity. Human capacity for love is creative. The ability to exercise that aspect of love is a continuation of God's own creative generosity. (2335)

Marriage therefore has two purposes: the happiness of the couple themselves and the sharing with the creator in bringing new life into the world. These cannot be separated without compromising the good of the marriage, the couple and their children. (2363)

The Church teaches, as does the Bible, that man and woman shall 'become one flesh'. Sexual acts are noble and honourable and they should be a source of joy and pleasure for both body and spirit. The Church also insists that sexual intercourse is only permissible within marriage and when it is open to the creation of new life. (2362)

Adultery is an offence against the sanctity and dignity of marriage, and is always essentially wrong. It is an injustice, a failure to honour the marriage commitment. It damages the partners, the marriage, and the children. (2380f.)

The danger of adultery is ever present; fallen human nature is always prone to temptation. So Jesus in the gospels says that those who look upon others with lust are already guilty of adultery in their hearts (Matt 5:28).

The Church is determined to protect sex as the tremendous and dignified gift from God that it has been from the beginning, too precious to be trivialized by temporary and uncommitted liaisons.

The Catechism quotes some beautiful words of St John Chrysostom advising young husbands to say to their wives 'I love you and prefer you to my life itself. For the present life is nothing and my most ardent dream is to spend it with you in such a way that we may be assured of not being separated in the life reserved for us.' Church teaching on marriage aims at helping husband and wife to do just this. (2365)

Q.78 The sixth commandment speaks of the importance of chastity. What does chastity mean?

A. Chastity is sometimes misunderstood as meaning a complete absence of sexual activity. In fact it means being true to our state in life whether we are single, married or celibate and conducting our sexual relationships with dignity and responsibility. No one form of chastity is superior to another. (2367)

Through chastity we learn to control our passions rather than allowing them to control us. Unless we do this we are submitting ourselves to a slavery that cannot make us happy. Mastering our passions, however, is not easy and requires constant effort, prayer and obedience to the commandments. It can be especially difficult during adolescence. (2338ff.)

Those engaged to marry are called on to practise chastity by waiting until they are married before they enjoy full sexual intimacy. A time of engagement should be a time of concentrating on other aspects of the relationship when the couple help each other to develop mutual respect. Nowadays an increasing number of couples claim the right to a 'trial marriage' before fully committing themselves. Such liaisons are forbidden by the Church, which insists that sexual intercourse is only right when a couple have totally given themselves to each other in marriage. (2350)

Offences listed against chastity in the Catechism include:

lust, the desire for sexual pleasure ignoring both the good of the other person and any thought of procreation;

masturbation, which seeks selfish pleasure outside the sexual relationship, which is essentially one of mutual and unselfish giving. However, the Catechism points out that guilt here may be lessened by immaturity, force of habit, or psychological factors;

fornication, when a man and woman who are not married have sexual
intercourse;

pornography, which degrades the human being;

prostitution, which reduces a person to an instrument of pleasure for
another; and

rape, which violates human integrity and is always essentially evil
no matter what the circumstances. (2351ff.)

Dealing with homosexuality in this section, and basing its teaching
on Scripture, the Catechism says that all men and women who feel
sexually attracted to another of their own sex must also be chaste.
Although the psychological causes of homosexuality are largely not
understood, any physical homosexual acts are considered by the Church
to be against the natural law and 'gravely disordered'. Under no
circumstances can they be approved. (2357)

However, the Catechism says that many do not choose their sexual
orientation. Being homosexual is often a trial for the Christian. One way
forward is to unite him- or herself with the suffering of Jesus on the
cross. The Catechism condemns any form of discrimination against
homosexuals and urges that they should always be treated with compassion, respect and sensitivity. (2358)

Q.79 Are all forms of birth control forbidden by the Church?

A. The Church has constantly taught that every act of sexual intercourse must be open to new life. God's plan is seen as uniting the marriage act (the couple becoming one flesh) with the procreation of
children. The Church teaches that this link may not be broken. Having
children is a natural fruit of married life. Children are a gift from God
allowing the married couple to share in his creative fatherhood. (2368)

The Catechism changes nothing about this traditional teaching and
says that every form of artificial birth control and any action taken to
prevent conception, such as sterilization, is always evil, no matter what
the motives or intention. These actions also break the marriage promise
made by the husband and wife to give themselves fully to each other.
No other area of church discipline has caused such controversy and
difficulty, and it has often been criticized by both those inside and

outside the Church. But the Catechism says it is not possible to fully understand the responsibility of bringing children into the world in this life, only in the life to come. (2371)

However, church teaching does not forbid natural family planning, using the period when a woman is infertile, as this does not go against nature. Also it recommends that, at times, husband and wife should abstain from sex. This may even enrich their relationship by making them more tender to each other. (2370)

Although large families have traditionally been seen as a blessing from God, parents should be responsible about the number of children they have. (2372)

Q.80 How does the Church regard test-tube babies and other scientific techniques to help infertile couples to have children?

A. All attempts to conceive a child other than through sexual intercourse between a married couple are forbidden by the Church. This is because, as mentioned in the previous answer, the Church teaches there is an unbreakable link between the sex act and procreation designed by God. One may not be separated from the other. Addressing those who are unable to have children, the Church recognizes the pain and suffering that this can cause and encourages research that will help overcome this. The Catechism points out however that no one has a right to a child; a child is not a piece of property, but a gift from God. (2375, 2376, 2378)

All test-tube conceptions, and all techniques that involve any person other than the husband or wife, are gravely wrong. These include using the sperm or egg from a donor or a surrogate mother. These techniques deprive the child of its right to be born to a father and mother he or she knows and who are married to each other. (2377)

Even if only the husband and wife are involved in some kind of technique to have a baby other than through sexual intercourse, such as artificial insemination, this is still wrong but less so. The Catechism quotes Pope Paul VI in *Humanae Vitae* where he says 'This is, perhaps, less reprehensible, yet remains morally unacceptable'. This is because such parents are not producing the child in the natural and fully self-giving way designed by God the creator. The Catechism says that involving scientists and doctors in producing new life gives them too much power and control over human life.

In the Christian community no one is truly without a family, as the Church should be home and family to all, especially those who 'labour and are heavily burdened'.

Q.81 Is divorce ever allowed by the Church?

A. The Church teaches that divorce is a 'grave offence against the natural law'. It breaks the contract by which the couple have freely agreed to live together until death. If either of the parties marries again, even if the union is recognized in civil law, the offence is even more serious. Divorce is also wrong because of the damage it causes to the deserted partner, the family and the whole community. It is described as a 'plague on society'. (2384, 2385)

Sometimes however, one of the parties is an innocent victim in a divorce. In this case they have not broken the moral law. There is a great difference between a person who has tried to keep faithful to the marriage vow but is unjustly abandoned and a person who deliberately destroys a valid marriage. (2386)

In all cases of divorce the Church urges its pastors to do all they can to help the people involved and not to make them feel cut off from the Church. Where a person is an innocent victim and does not marry again, there is no bar to their receiving Holy Communion.

Other offences against marriage include polygamy. This is contrary to the natural law because married love should be total, unique and exclusive. Obviously any man who has many wives faces great difficulty should he wish to become a Christian. Although he can no longer practise polygamy after his conversion, he is bound to take care of all his previous wives and children. (2387)

Incest is also forbidden by this commandment as is any sexual abuse of children or young people. (2388)

Couples who decide to live together as husband and wife without getting married are breaking the moral law and damaging the whole concept of family life. Sexual intercourse outside marriage is always a grave sin and excludes the people involved from receiving Holy Communion. (2390)

Although the Church does not permit divorce, it does sometimes issue a decree of nullity; that is, a solemn declaration that, despite any appearance to the contrary, in the case of a particular couple, no real marriage ever existed (see Question 54).

Q.82 What is forbidden by the seventh commandment?

A. This commandment, which simply says 'You shall not steal' is used by the Church as the basis for a wide range of social teaching. The key concept is justice, and anything that is unjust, whether in personal relationships, work, business, or national and international dealings, is forbidden. There are lengthy passages in the Catechism on rights and duties at work and on political systems and Christian responsibility to the poor.

The seventh commandment also reminds us that the earth and all its fruits were created by God for all human beings and we must do what we can to see that all get their fair share. We certainly have a right to private property and goods but we should be careful not to use them selfishly, simply concentrating on our own needs. We are only stewards of our possessions and have a duty to see that others do not go short of what they need because we refuse to share what we can. To do this and help society develop in the right way we need, above all, to increase our awareness of God. (2402ff.)

In dealing specifically with theft, that is, taking anything that belongs to another, the Catechism includes deliberately failing to return things that have been lent, forcing prices up, evading just taxes, forging cheques or invoices, falsifying expenses, failing to do our work properly, not honouring business contracts and damaging other people's property. If we have stolen anything we are obliged to return it or make recompense. However it is not wrong to take something that is absolutely essential for survival, such as basic food or clothing, if there is no other way of getting it and it is being unreasonably refused. (2408f.)

Some commentators have expressed surprise that the Catechism seems to forbid gambling. It is only against excessive gambling, the kind that becomes addictive and could result in the person losing all they have or damaging themselves or their dependants. Cheating at any game is also considered sinful if it causes someone to lose large sums of money, or more than they can afford. (2413)

Q.83 Is poverty considered a virtue, and what does the Catechism say about responsibilities towards the poor?

A. God gave the world and its fruits to be shared equally among all his children, yet great deprivation and poverty continue to exist, while others have far more than they could ever need. All rich countries therefore have a responsibility to share their God-given resources with the poorer nations and assist them in any way they can. Poverty is partly caused because many, particularly in the more developed nations, are unwilling to do this and are failing in justice by keeping what is not truly and fully theirs. (2437ff.)

Jesus taught his followers that they should have a special love for those lacking in worldly goods and who find it a struggle just to stay alive. He himself chose to be identified with those who had least in the material sense. Those who have, should always be ready to share with those who have not. Jesus tells us through the gospels that if we have two coats we should be prepared to give one to a person who has none. Those of us who are well able to take care of ourselves have a responsibility to help those who are not so blessed. Helping the poor is so important that the gospels imply that it is by what they have done for the poor that Jesus Christ will recognize his chosen ones. Anyone in doubt about responsibilities, not just to the poor, but to all in need should re-read Matthew's Gospel, chapter 25, verses 31 to 46. Here we learn that the corporal works of mercy, or the way that we can demonstrate our Christian faith, is to do all we can for those less fortunate than ourselves. This includes feeding the hungry, visiting the sick and imprisoned, clothing the naked. How can we love the God we cannot see unless we love the neighbour we can see? (2443)

St Paul develops this teaching by saying that we even might have a duty to work so as to be able to give to those in need (Eph 4:28), and St John Chrysostom condemned those who do not share their goods with the poor as 'stealing from them and depriving them of life'. Sharing is not charity, because it is something that we owe those in need. (2446)

The Church has always shown its love for the poor by working to help them. This is so important in Christian teaching that, according to St John Chrysostom, those who share the bread in Holy Communion dishonour the table if they are not also willing to share their own food with those in need. In the section on prayer the Catechism reminds us that as we pray the Lord's Prayer and ask for our daily bread, we are called to help all who are hungry. They are all part of the one human family, our family. The one bread is for everyone. (2828ff.)

Jesus often praises the poor and says that those who are not attached to worldly goods stand a better chance of achieving eternal life than the rich, who find their satisfaction and comfort in their possessions. In his Sermon on the Mount he said 'Blessed are the poor in spirit, for theirs is the Kingdom of heaven'.

We should remember that when speaking of the poor, the Church does not only mean those who lack material goods but also those who lack cultural and religious riches, and calls on us to share our material and spiritual goods out of love for each other. (2448)

Q.84 Does the Church favour any one political system over the others?

A. Although Church authorities do not directly involve themselves in party politics – lay members are expected to do that where they can – the Church has strong views on political systems. As its mission is to protect the good of all human beings, the Church is against any political system which devalues human persons or in any way restricts their basic rights. God created the world and its goods for all, and governments should recognize this in their legislation. The good of the human person comes first. This applies to all political systems. In capitalism, making money is often put before all else, reducing people to a kind of slavery. This can lead to idolizing money, and as Scripture reminds us, 'You cannot serve God and Mammon' (Luke 16:13). The Catechism points out that the human being has many needs and desires that cannot be satisfied only by money. (2442, 2425)

Communism is also rejected by the Church because it places the good of the State before the good of the individual, whose rights are totally subjected to the common good. As a consequence of this it also denies the existence of God, who has made people in his image and likeness who should therefore be respected as individuals with specific human rights, and it penalizes those who insist on following this belief.

The Catechism also addresses international politics. Central to church teaching here is that the rich nations must help the poor. Those who have natural and God-given resources which allow them to build and grow, have a responsibility to those who do not have these riches and who are accumulating huge debts, often because of unjust interest charges. Excessive amounts of money and effort are also absorbed by the scandalous international arms race, when they could be used to relieve world-wide poverty, starvation and death from diseases that could be cured if there were sufficient resources. (2437ff.)

Direct aid, however, is not enough. It is certainly the right immediate response to any disaster, but it does not in the long term solve a country's economic problems. To do this it is necessary to help the particular country improve its economy so that the people can eventually help themselves. Meanwhile all those in deprived countries who are working to improve conditions should be supported by governments and any individuals who can help.

Although the Church favours no particular political system, it teaches that the only way a society can develop fully and justly is by recognizing and accepting the existence of God and his laws. (2440, 2442)

The Catechism says that although the clergy should not involve themselves directly in politics, the Church is entitled to make judgements about social and economic matters when human rights or the salvation of the soul is involved.

Q.85 What does the seventh commandment say about work?

A. Significant advances were made, during the nineteenth century, in the social teaching of the Church. The industrial revolution had introduced many new concepts and practices in the world of work. The Church was concerned that neither the employee nor the employer should be exploited. (2427)

The Catechism sets out the rights and duties of both employers and employees. People have a duty to work for three reasons: to support themselves, their families, and those who depend on them; to help the community, especially those less fortunate; and to develop and share the talents that God has given each one.

St Paul said 'If a man does not work neither shall he eat'. He meant of course those who refused to work, not those who could not find employment. Work helps people fulfil their human potential. It involves us all in sharing God's continuing work of creation.

Employers, for their part, should consider the good of their employees and not be concerned only with making profits. Obviously some profits are legitimate, and are even essential, if the business is to continue and to provide further employment. Workers are entitled to a just wage sufficient to provide a dignified livelihood for the employee and his or her family. Refusing to pay a just wage is a grave offence against the seventh commandment. Employers are also urged not to discriminate against any individual or group. Jobs should be open to both men and women, able and disabled, native and immigrants alike. (2434)

Work can often involve a conflict of interest between employers and workers. The Church urges that, where possible, these differences should be solved by negotiation and arbitration. Employees have a fundamental right to form trades unions in order to protect their interests and to negotiate with management for improved pay or working conditions when necessary. If all else fails, then workers have the right to strike. However, such action must not involve violence and can only be taken if the purpose of the strike is to improve working conditions or some other aspect of the common good. (2435)

Unemployment damages both the individual and the family. But people are not worth any less because they have no paid job. Human dignity should not depend on being employed. Those particularly who, through no fault of their own, are unemployed, need to be shown the love and concern of the whole Christian community. (2436)

Q.86 Does this commandment say anything about animals?

A. When God created the world he made humans the 'stewards of creation'; they were to be in charge of all other creatures. Everything was to be used for the common good. Men and women were charged equally with this responsibility and consequently they have a duty to see that all resources are used in ways that will not deprive others or damage their quality of life, either at present or in the future. (2415, 2457)

Animals are a very important part of this rich inheritance. 'By their very existence they bless and glorify God', the Catechism says.

Therefore they are to be treated with the greatest of care, following the example of St Francis of Assisi, renowned for his love of the animal kingdom. Animals should never be made to suffer or die cruelly or unnecessarily. However, since they exist, like all other creatures, for the good of humankind, it is not wrong to kill them in order to provide food and clothing. Certain reasonable experiments on animals are allowed if their object is to prevent disease or to save human lives. (2416)

However, we must not let our concern for animals allow us to place them above human beings either by giving them the degree of love and affection that is intended for humans, or by lavishly spending money on them which could help people in need. (2417f.)

Q.87 What does the eighth commandment mean by 'false witness'?

A. It means any kind of untruthfulness or lack of honesty in word or action. This includes all kinds of lies, even minor ones or 'white lies', hypocrisy and perjury. Lying is wrong because it goes against the purpose of speech, which is to communicate the truth to others, not to mislead them. God is truth and to live in him is to live in truth. If society is to function properly people must be able to trust each other. Lack of honesty obviously helps to destroy this trust and undermines the whole society. (2464, 2470)

Lying in small matters is only a venial sin. It becomes a grave offence if it seriously damages another person in some way by leading them into grave error or by harming them, for example causing them to lose their job. (2483ff.)

This commandment also forbids any words or actions that could harm another's reputation or good name, which is difficult to restore. This goes so far as to include rash judgements of another, without sufficient proof, or making someone's faults or failings public. It is often too easy to run a person down or join in unfavourable gossip about them. As far as possible we should give them the benefit of the doubt and be ready to find good in what they do. (2477)

On the other hand, we should not go too far the other way and praise or flatter people who we know are doing wrong even if they are far more powerful than we are. Sometimes even by remaining silent in such situations we can appear to consent to wrongdoings. (2480)

Although we should never tell an untruth even for what appear to be good reasons, such as preserving a friendship, we are not always bound to disclose all we know, especially to someone who has no right to the particular information, or if what we say could cause scandal. We should be especially careful in gossiping about other people's private lives. Anyone who by lying causes harm, especially to another's good name, is bound to make amends. When this is not possible publicly then it should be done in private. (2479, 2487)

This brings us to the question of the circumstances under which a person has the right to withhold information. The Church has taught that a priest may never disclose anything he has been told in confession no matter how serious the reasons for doing so. This is known as 'the seal of confession'. Others who have a right to withhold information disclosed to them in confidence are doctors, lawyers and soldiers. Only if they have reason to believe that by refusing to give the relevant information someone could be seriously or unjustly harmed, can they break this trust. (2490)

One area included in this commandment which might not be obvious is the need for Christian witness, to stand up for one's faith. Those who believe must never be ashamed of being open about it. The supreme example of Christian witness is of course martyrdom, dying to defend one's belief. (2473)

Q.88 What does this commandment say about the mass media and the truth?

A. The Catechism recognizes that one of the greatest influences on the lives of people throughout the world today is the mass media, especially television. What the mass media say is increasingly important. They provide most of us with the information on which to base our view of what is happening in the world and, in some cases, on which to base our moral judgements. It is clear, therefore, that what we see, hear or read should give us a true picture of what is happening. This lays a particular responsibility on writers, producers and editors to tell the truth. They should never lower themselves to write malicious or false gossip or scandal which can destroy someone's reputation or good name. People's privacy must be respected.

The Catechism goes on to say that those who use the media are responsible for what and how they watch, listen or read. Excessive television viewing, for example, can cause people to become too passive, lose sight of real life and be distracted into a world of fantasy. Some programmes also encourage voyeurism, which is unpleasant and destructive. (2493, 2496)

Those in government have a responsibility to keep a sharp eye on the mass media and see that they do not misuse their considerable power. If there is any breach of truth, those in authority must take suitable action. No one should be allowed to manipulate public opinion, especially in totalitarian states where those in power can be unscrupulous in controlling opinion by using the media and destroying freedom of thought or speech. (2498, 2500)

The arts are another channel of communication that reaches many people. Artistic ability is a talent given by God to some, to be used for the good and inspiration of others. It can communicate experiences that are beyond words. In essence it is a form of heart speaking to heart.

Sacred art has long been a major source for the communication of religious teaching and truths. European culture would be much the poorer without the great art, architecture, writing and music that continue to witness to the faith of generations. The Catechism says it is important that those in authority in the Church should continue to encourage all forms of religious art, both old and new. However, they are also reminded that any object which does not truly promote the truth and beauty of the Christian faith should not be displayed in any place of worship or liturgical celebration. (2502)

Q.89 The ninth and tenth commandments forbid coveting. What does this word mean? If both commandments forbid the same thing, why are they divided into two?

A. To covet means to want something belonging to another so deeply that it dominates our lives. We set our heart on it above all else. The word comes from the Latin *cupiditas*, which means 'greed'. The ninth commandment refers to an intense desire to possess someone else's spouse and to have sexual relations with them when we have no right to it. The tenth commandment refers to all material goods. But both commandments have the same root, which is envy and greed. The flesh struggling against the spirit is something we constantly experience because human nature has been weakened by original sin. (2515f.)

The actual wording of the ninth commandment in the Bible is 'You shall not covet your neighbour's house, you shall not covet your neighbour's wife, or his manservant or his ox, or his ass, or anything that is his' (Exodus 20:17). The tenth commandment is very similar: 'You shall not covet anything that is your neighbour's. You shall not desire your neighbour's house, his field, or his manservant or his maidservant, or his ox, or his ass, or anything that is his' (Deut 5:21). The difference is that the ninth commandment includes the word 'wife'. When these commandments were originally drawn up, at the time of Moses, a man's wife tended to be regarded as part of his possessions. The commandments were subsequently split into two to make the point that, in Christian teaching, a woman is not simply a chattel or possession, but a person in her own right.

The ninth commandment therefore has been treated by the Church as principally forbidding any lustful desires for another person's spouse. Jesus himself was very strict about this and said 'Everyone who looks at a woman lustfully has already committed adultery with her in his heart' (Matt 5:28). Addressing this commandment, the Catechism says that lustful desires can be overcome by a constant attempt to find and follow God and his will, by rejecting impure thoughts and by regular prayer. (2520)

Modesty also plays an important part. This involves not flaunting our bodies, or wearing indecent or revealing clothing. Advertisements also should not exploit the human body, and the media generally have a responsibility not to show intimate parts of the body or human acts that are essentially private. Voyeurism is unhealthy and unchristian. (2521)

Modern society is often in conflict with these attitudes and prefers to be morally permissive. Permissiveness is based on a mistaken idea of freedom. True freedom can only be achieved by accepting the moral law which provides freedom for all. Otherwise there is a danger that what we think is freedom is simply slavery to one passion or another. Jesus taught that 'Blessed are the pure of heart, for they shall see God' (Matt 5:8). (2526)

Q.90 Does the tenth commandment mean that we must never want something that belongs to another person?

A. No, it does not. There is nothing wrong in admiring another's possessions or in wishing that they belonged to us. Such a desire only becomes wrong and is forbidden by this commandment when it grows into envy, greed or avarice. It scarcely needs the Catechism to warn us, as it does, that if we set our hearts on making money we will never have enough. Defining envy, the Catechism quotes St Augustine who called it 'the diabolical sin'. It was because the devil envied the friendship between the creator and the first humans that he tempted them to commit sin by disobeying God and damaging their relationship with him. (2537, 2538ff.)

Envy also comes from pride, which has no place in Christian life as Christians are called by Jesus to be humble. Envy makes people sad when they see others justly prosper. True Christian love demands that they should be glad for them. Envy springs from the false idea that material possessions alone can bring true happiness. As the Catechism often reminds us, only our relationship with God can do that. It is the Holy Spirit who satisfied our hearts' desires. Only by abandoning ourselves to God's goodness can we be free of anxiety.

Happiness comes from freeing ourselves from undue attachment to worldly goods and setting our sights on eternal life with God. Jesus preached the importance of that detachment in his Sermon on the Mount, when he said 'Blessed are the poor in spirit, for theirs is the Kingdom of heaven'. Jesus urged those who listened to him to renounce their worldly goods and follow him. Wealth, or at least a reasonable sufficiency of money, is not condemned, provided it is justly acquired. It is good and helps to make our life on earth comfortable, but Scripture warns that those who devote themselves totally to worldly comforts will not achieve the Kingdom of heaven. (2548ff.)

PART FOUR

CHRISTIAN PRAYER

Q.91 What is prayer?

A. Because God has made us in his own image, with intelligence and free will, we are able to know him and to acknowledge him. From the human point of view, then, prayer is the willing and humble recognition and honouring of God as our creator. St Augustine defined prayer as 'The raising of one's mind and heart to God, or the requesting of good things from God'. The Catechism says that prayer springs from our heart; that is our inner self.

In the Jewish Scriptures, the Old Testament, the history of humanity is seen to be the history of prayer. Our first parents walked and conversed with God in Eden. Cain had to answer to God for his brother's death. Noah, who 'walked with God', had his offering accepted, and Abraham, above all, is seen as a man who intimately conversed with God, willing to obey him even to the sacrifice of his own son. When God showed him that human sacrifice is not acceptable to him, a long tradition of animal and vegetable sacrifice began which lasted right down to the time of Jesus. The book of Exodus describes Moses as one who spoke to God 'face to face, as one speaks with a friend'. (2568ff., 2576)

The divine presence was symbolized, first by the Ark of the Covenant and later by the Jerusalem Temple. The people prostrated themselves in prayer before these symbols of God's presence. And the prophets, too, while trying to turn their straying people's hearts back to God, interceded for them with the Almighty. (2581ff.)

With the coming of the great kings, David and his son Solomon, worship was raised to new heights with the composing of the psalms. These too were at the heart of Christ's prayer, but with him, as we shall see, prayer was raised to a new level. (2559f., 2578f., 2598)

Q.92 How can we pray? Are there any practical things we should do?

A. Prayer is talking and listening to God; relating to him. It is essential if we are to be truly Christian. Like any relationship, it requires effort, energy, time and space. If the relationship is to grow we must be ready not just to talk, to share our innermost desires and self, but also to listen. Although the human heart naturally desires to pray, to communicate with God who has created it for himself, it is not always easy to do this. Many things tend to prevent us, as we shall see.

The first essential requirement for prayer is the right attitude to God – a genuine, heartfelt desire to be in communication with him, open not just to hear his will for us, but to accept it. If our hearts are far from God, unwilling to accept his will, our prayers, no matter how elegant and frequent, are empty. God does not require golden words but golden hearts. We do not have to worry about finding the right words, the Holy Spirit will help us to do that if we ask. Sometimes words are not necessary at all. It is the heart that prays, that deep centre of self that only God can know, the real us without the mask. (2626, 2665)

Prayer can mean just taking the ordinary things of our daily life, however insignificant they may seem, and offering them to God. Or simple words may be enough. One of the shortest prayers is to call on the Holy Name of Jesus. This we can do at any time under any circumstances. We can also call on the Holy Spirit, without whom we cannot pray at all, and say 'Come, Holy Spirit, fill the hearts of your faithful and kindle in them the fire of your love'. (2668ff., 2745, 2752)

Scripture plays an important part in prayer life and regular reading from the Bible as we pray will help us communicate with God. When we pray we speak to God and tell him our desires. When we read the Scriptures, his inspired Word, we listen to him. (2705, 2762)

We have to learn to pray. Our first teachers are our parents, and children need the example of regular family prayer. Teaching children some simple prayers by heart can be helpful but it is important that, as they learn the words, they also are helped to understand the meaning of what they say. (2685)

In private and personal prayer we might find it helpful to have some corner or space in our home, no matter how small, with a crucifix, statue or sacred image which can lead our hearts and minds to God. (2691)

Q.93 Is prayer essentially personal: speaking with God one-to-one?

A. No. We also learn to develop our prayer life through our relationship with the Church and our clergy, as well as with other people. Priests have a special responsibility to lead their people to God, and this must include helping them to pray. Spiritual directors can also help in our prayer life, provided that we choose the right person – a man or woman who has a healthy spiritual life themselves and has experience in the guidance of souls. (2655, 2686)

Jesus said 'Wherever two or three are gathered in my name, there I am among them'. What better recommendation for group prayer could we need? Prayer in the family is also important, especially when the children are young. Some may find it helpful to join one of the increasing number of prayer groups, which the Catechism calls 'driving forces for renewal in the prayer life of the whole Church'. The greatest experience of group prayer is undoubtedly the coming together of the parish or other community for the celebration of the Mass. (2689)

One of the qualities essential for a thriving prayer life is a great patience and perseverance. As Jesus taught in his parable of the insistent widow, it is necessary to 'pray without ceasing' (Luke 18:1–8). Strong faith is also required, believing that God will listen to us and that with him all things are possible to those who believe. Faith can move mountains.

Prayer should become so much part of us that we can pray at any time and in any place. As St Gregory Nazianzen wrote, 'We must remember God more often than we draw breath'. We are called on to pray constantly. But we cannot do this unless we set aside some special time for prayer. This can be at the start or the end of the day, before and after meals, or joining in the daily prayer of the Church (the Liturgy of the Hours).

Although it is possible to pray anywhere, some places make praying easier and help us to concentrate. Obviously a church building, a chapel or a prayer-room is best when we are sharing in liturgical or community prayer. There also we will often find the reserved Sacrament and so be able to adore the Real Presence of Jesus. Other places where we can develop our relationship with God are retreat houses, public shrines or places of pilgrimage, associated with Christ or one of the saints. (2691)

Q.94 What are the main difficulties that we encounter when we try to pray?

A. Prayer is essential to our spiritual life. As with any part of spiritual life, it is not easy. The spirit has to fight against the devil, who tries to turn us from God and his love, and also against our human nature, which is weakened by original sin. (We should be encouraged by the story in the gospels of how, on the night before the passion of Jesus, even his closest friends could not stay awake to pray with him at that vital moment. Jesus did not condemn or criticize them for their failure.) Prayer is also made more difficult because our society is highly materialistic. Activities such as prayer do not add to the Gross National Product. Our life-style generally is highly active and busy and it is difficult to make time for prayer, which is essential if we are to communicate with God. One of the most common problems in praying is distraction. We find our thoughts wandering to other things. The only way to deal with this is to turn our minds back to God as often as necessary. Sometimes in our prayer we will experience spiritual dryness; we feel separated from God. In this case we simply have to cling to our faith. Other problems that can stunt prayer life are weakness of faith, a refusal to be humble before God, or carelessness in our spiritual life. We can also be discouraged if it seems that no matter how hard we pray we are not answered or even heard. But we have the assurance of Jesus himself that the Father listens to all that we ask. He answers us, but not always in the way we expect. (2725, 2733, 2734ff.)

Q.95 What are the psalms?

A. The psalms are songs of praise and the greatest expressions of prayer in the Old Testament. They are a collection of some 150 sacred songs, originally composed for group or choral singing, and attributed to the great King David. As a youth, David had slain the Philistine, Goliath, in single combat and so became a folk-hero, and eventually, as king of Israel, ruled from 1000 to 961 BC. It was his idea to build a temple for the worship of God in Jerusalem although this did not happen until after his death. It is certain that the psalms were sung in Temple worship, as they are to this day in the worship of the synagogue. (2585ff.)

In the psalms, the *mirabilia Dei*, the wonderful deeds of God, are remembered and celebrated. They both recall the saving events of the past, such as the Exodus, and express a hope for future deliverance from ill and for the eventual coming of the Messiah.

Jesus himself made his prayer from the psalms, reciting one (Psalm 22) even as he died on the cross: 'My God, my God, why hast thou forsaken me?' (Mark 15:34). (2597)

Together with other Scripture passages, the psalms make up a large part of Christian worship today. They are used in the liturgy of the Mass, for instance, as the responsorial psalms which separate the readings in the Liturgy of the Word. They form the major part of the great monastic Liturgy of the Hours, the Divine Office, in which the passing of time is sanctified by prayer seven times a day. This is said by all religious, priests, nuns and brothers throughout the entire world, and ever more frequently by lay people in parish churches.

Some of the older psalms are somewhat bloodthirsty and primitive in character. Nevertheless, when prayed and meditated upon in faith, and especially when sung, they can provide a deep spiritual nourishment both for the individual and the community. (2588)

Although the psalms originally arose from the Jewish communities of the Holy Land and the Diaspora (those scattered abroad), they apply to all times and all peoples in their sufferings, their hopes and their faith that God has saved them.

Q.96 To whom do we pray?

A. All prayers are addressed to God or to Mary or one of the other saints. For Christians, prayers to the Father are often directed through the Son, 'through Christ Our Lord'. Jesus is quoted in the gospels: 'No one comes to the Father except through me' (John 14:6). As God incarnate, that is God made man, he is the 'natural' access point for humanity with God. We pray to the Father as our creator, to the Son as our redeemer and to the Holy Spirit who blesses us and makes us holy. It is the Holy Spirit who inspires us and helps us to pray. The constant prayer of the Church is 'Come, Holy Spirit, fill the hearts of your faithful'.

Prayers which are offered to the saints are not the adoration which is due to God alone, but a recognition of the special place in the Communion of Saints which the blessed, those whom the Church officially recognizes as being in heaven, hold. We invoke them so that they may intercede for us with the Almighty.

Mary, the Mother of God, has a special place among the saints. In her prayer 'be it done to me according to your word', when she was told by the angel that she had been chosen to be the mother of God, she completely surrendered to the will of God. An ancient tradition honours her with the *Ave Maria*, the Hail Mary, in which she is asked to pray for 'us sinners'. (2617ff., 2673ff.)

In the Church, many men and women in religious orders have consecrated their lives to prayer, constantly interceding with God on behalf of all his people. Through them the spiritual life of the whole Church is constantly refreshed and enlivened. (2687)

Q.97 What did Jesus teach about prayer?

A. The gospels show Jesus as a man of profound prayer both in public and in private. Again and again he is described as withdrawing to the desert or the mountain to pray to his Father. All the key events in his public life are preceded by prayer: his baptism in the Jordan, the calling of his apostles, the transfiguration, and his passion and death when he prayed his great prayer of forgiveness: 'Father, forgive them, for they know not what they do' (Luke 23:34). Even though Jesus is God, his prayer to the Father is always characterized by the most important element in any human dealings with God: humility.

Because of the mystery of the Incarnation, Christ, being both true God and true man, can be seen to *be* the perfect prayer: Godhead and humanity united in his very being. In his prayer, Jesus did not just pray for himself, his apostles and their mission, but for all humanity and all creation. In offering himself in obedience to the Father, he brings with him all of humanity. The Catechism quotes the letter to the Hebrews: 'In the days of his flesh, Jesus offered up prayers and supplications, with loud cries and tears, to him who was able to save him from death, and he was heard for his godly fear. Although he was a son, he learned obedience through what he suffered, and being made perfect, he became the source of eternal salvation to all who obey him' (Hebrews 5:7–9). (2606)

In teaching his disciples about prayer, Jesus first of all stresses that all prayer must spring from a converted heart; you must be reconciled with your brother or sister before you bring your gift to the altar. This is so important that if we realize that we are not reconciled with somebody, we must leave our gift while we make amends. Prayer must be sincere, not empty phrases. This in turn will allow the prayer to be faith-full: 'knock and it shall be opened to you.' 'Whatever you ask in prayer, believe that you will receive it, and you will' and again, 'all things are possible to one who believes'. Even when our prayers seem to go unanswered, Jesus taught that we must never give up. (2608)

When the disciples asked Jesus to teach them to pray, he gave them that prayer which we know today as the Lord's Prayer, a prayer which is unique and unsurpassed as a model of all prayer.

St Augustine is quoted on Jesus' prayer: 'He prays for us as our priest, prays in us as our head, and is prayed to by us as our God.' The peak and climax of all prayer is found in the great thanksgiving prayer of the Eucharist in which Christ gives himself totally to the Father and to his followers (see Question 48).

Q.98 Are our prayers always answered?

A. Perhaps the question should be 'Are our prayers always heard?', in which case, of course, the answer is yes, provided they are made with faith and humility. When it comes to praying for things we want ourselves, however, we tend to expect God not just to hear our prayers, but to answer them and to do as we ask. After all, Jesus did say 'knock and it shall be opened to you'. Nevertheless, it does seem that, sometimes, prayers go unanswered. Why is this? It is not a new problem. St James, in his epistle (chapter 4) explains: 'You ask and do not receive, because you ask wrongly . . .' Our reasons may not always be the best in God's sight. Clearly, God, who is all-knowing and all-wise, as well as all-loving, will not grant us something which he, in his infinite wisdom, knows will not be for our good, either in this life or the next. (2738ff.)

God rules all creation through those laws of nature which he himself established from all eternity. We can hardly expect him to change those laws just to suit our immediate needs. The whole of creation exists in the divine providence where 'all things work together unto good'.

Our prayer, if genuine, will be made with a heart attuned to the divine will. As Jesus taught us in the words of the Lord's Prayer, 'Thy will be done ...'. Just how that divine will may be accomplished will sometimes cause us perplexity and perhaps even suffering in the short term. Nevertheless, all genuine prayers to the Father will be heard, and answered, although often in ways that we may least expect or understand. Ultimately, the success or otherwise of our prayers will depend not on the number or eloquence of our words, but on the fervour of our souls.

It could be asked, why do we need to ask for anything in prayer if an all-wise God knows all our needs even before we express them? The answer is, of course, that God does not 'need' our prayers at all. Rather, when we have come to know God, we need to communicate with him, to express our dependence upon and love of him. We do this in prayer.

Jesus himself told his disciples, 'Whatever you ask the Father in my name, he will give it to you. This I command you, to love one another.' It is not by chance that his words on prayer to the Father are so closely linked with his command to love. (2739ff., 2779f.)

Q.99 What is the 'Hail Mary' and what is its importance?

A. Because of her unique position in the Communion of Saints, Mary, the Mother of God, has always been honoured in prayer. The most popular prayer to her is that known as the 'Hail Mary', or the Angelic Salutation:

Hail, Mary, full of grace,
the Lord is with thee.
Blessed art thou among women,
and blessed is the fruit of thy womb, Jesus.
Holy Mary, Mother of God,
pray for us sinners,
now and at the hour of our death. Amen.

The opening lines of this prayer are based on St Luke's account, in his Gospel, of the Annunciation, when the angel, Gabriel, is sent by God to invite Mary to be the mother of the redeemer. The angel is described as greeting her with the words 'Hail, full of grace. The Lord is with thee' (Luke 1:28). The words 'full of grace' indicate the complete sinlessness of Mary from the first moment of her existence. Further on in the same account, St Luke describes how Mary visited her cousin, Elizabeth, before the birth of her child, who was to be called John the Baptist. Elizabeth's greeting to Mary, 'Blessed art thou among women, and blessed is the fruit of thy womb' (Luke 1:42), is joined to that of the angel to form the first part of the prayer. The fruit of Mary's womb, Jesus the Messiah, is, of course, the reason why she is so blessed and has been honoured throughout the centuries. The Church adds the further lines, giving her the supreme title of Mother of God, and straight away calls on her as the great intercessor for 'us sinners' not only here and now, but also at that most crucial moment when we must pass from this life to the next and when, at our judgement, we may well have need of the powerful intercession of the Queen of all saints, on our behalf. (2676, 2677)

In the Western Church, the Middle Ages saw the development of the Rosary. This is a prayer-formula of meditation on the life and death of Jesus, composed mainly of the 'Hail Mary' repeated many times, as a popular substitute for the more complicated Liturgy of the Hours (the Divine Office). The recitation of the Rosary as a family prayer in the home is still popular in many parts of Europe. (2678)

Q.100 What is the Lord's Prayer?

A. The gospels say that when the disciples asked Jesus how to pray, he gave them the prayer that all Christians have used ever since: the Lord's Prayer or the 'Our Father'.

> Our Father who art in heaven,
> hallowed be thy name.
> Thy kingdom come.
> Thy will be done on earth, as it is in heaven.
> Give us this day our daily bread,
> and forgive us our trespasses,
> as we forgive those who trespass against us,
> and lead us not into temptation,
> but deliver us from evil. (2759)

This is the fundamental Christian prayer, and Tertullian, a

theologian of the second century, described it as 'the summary of the whole gospel'. St Thomas Aquinas said that in the Lord's Prayer we not only ask for the things we can rightly desire, but also in the sequence that they should be desired. (2761)

It is significant that Jesus used the word 'our' rather than 'my'. This was to teach his disciples that prayer is not only personal or private, but also public and corporate: the prayer of the whole body which is the Church.

The Lord's Prayer is so central to the whole teaching of Jesus that it is included in every major sacramental and liturgical ceremony in all Christian churches. (2768ff.)

When addressing his Father, Jesus used the Hebrew word *Abba* which is closer to the English word 'Daddy', and which indicates the trust and love of a child.

This model prayer asks that:

1 God's name be known and blessed everywhere. (2807ff.)
2 The Kingdom or reign of God be established in every human heart. (2816ff.)
3 God's will, that all should be saved through the divine love, should come about. (2822ff.)
4 God, in his goodness, would provide for all human needs, spiritual, and material. (2828ff.)
5 He should forgive us our sins, only insofar as we are ready to forgive those who have offended us. (2838ff.)
6 By his grace, we may be protected from falling into temptation, and from all those evils which the devil, the father of lies, constantly wishes upon all human beings, especially those who love the heavenly Father. (2846, 2850)

In some Christian traditions a final word of praise is added to the Lord's Prayer: 'For the kingdom, the power and the glory are yours, now and forever.' In the liturgy of the Mass, these words are spoken by the congregation before they receive Holy Communion. (2855f.)

And finally: What does the word 'Amen' mean?

A. Amen is an ancient Hebrew word. It originally meant 'certainly'. It is clearly, then, a word of agreement. By tradition it is used at the end of many prayers, expressing the *fiat* of those making, or wishing to be associated with, the contents of the prayer. By adding it to the Lord's Prayer we make our own that which has come to us from God himself. AMEN! (2856)